004.
H38678
A.B.
£9-99

OCR Computing for AS Level
F451 Computer Fundamentals
A Revision Guide

Alan Milosevic, Dorothy Williams

All questions and model answers © OCR

Published by Bagatelle Publications Ltd 2012

Published by Bagatelle Publications Ltd

http://www.bagatelle.com/

First published 2012

Printed in the United Kingdom

Set using LATEX. Font 10pt Minion Pro.

Contents

Introduction

This revision guide has been written specifically to support work done throughout the year in F451 - Computer Fundamentals. It is not intended to replace a good text book but when used properly will provide an excellent supplement. The revision guide is divided into chapters and sections. Each chapter and section reflect divisions in the original OCR specification for F451. Notes are distributed throughout the guide immediately after each section heading. These notes are then followed by a range of questions taken directly from OCR past papers, together with the examiner's mark scheme solutions. The questions and answers are intended to fulfil a dual purpose. They provide excellent notes and they also provide a definitive guide to the type of questions asked on the F451 paper with exemplars of the answers you should provide.

All of the questions are taken from OCR past papers. In each instance the question number and paper are displayed together with the number of marks awarded for a fully correct answer. The answers are provided by the OCR mark scheme for the particular paper. Many of these answers are given in bullet point form. You should assume that each bullet point is worth one mark, with the proviso that if the bullet point contains an ellipsis (...), the text following the ellipsis expanding upon or providing an explanation for the first part of the text is also worth one mark.

The student who works his or her way through this book carefully reading the notes and past paper questions and answers will give themselves an excellent opportunity to consolidate and review the material learned during the course.

Components of a Computer System

1.1 Define the terms hardware, software, input device, storage device and output device

Hardware is the physical part of a computer system.

Software consists of programs, routines and procedures which can be run on a computer system.

Input devices are peripheral devices that can accept data presented in the appropriate machine readable form, decode it and transmit it as as electrical impulses to the CPU. Examples include keyboards, mice, digital cameras, microphones and touch screens.

Storage devices are memory devices used to store programs, applications, operating systems and user data when the computer is switched off and for later retrieval. Examples include hard disk drives, CDROM drives re-writable CD-RW, DVDs (R and RW) and USB memory sticks.

Output devices translate signals from the computer into a human readable form or into a form suitable for re-processing by the computer at a later stage. Examples include printers, screens, plotters and speakers.

Define the term hardware. [F451 Q1 Jan 2010 (1)]

- The physical parts of a computer system

Some hardware items are called peripherals. Explain what is meant by a peripheral. (2)

- External to the computer/attached to the computer/outside the processor/connects to computer
- E.g. printer to output hard copy

Define the term software. (1)

- Instructions, programs (to make the hardware work)

State what is meant by an input device. [F451 Q1 Jun 2009 (1)]

- Hardware used to put data into a computer

State what is meant by an output device. (1)

- Hardware used to get information from a computer

A supermarket checkout terminal has both input and output devices. State two input devices and two output devices which would be used at the checkout. In each case state why they would be used. (2,2,2,2)

Input

- Barcode reader …to input product ID printed on product
- Keyboard …to manually input data if barcode will not read
- Automatic scales …to input weight of fresh produce
- Chip & Pin reader/card reader …to input card details
- Keypad …to input PIN for card

Output

- Screen …to show details of objects scanned/current state of transaction
- Printer …to print till receipt
- Beeper …to indicate valid reading of code

A library directs all members to an area where they can have their loans input into the computer system. The membership number is read from the members card. Describe two ways that the membership number can be input to the computer system. [F451 Q5 Jan 2010 (2,2)]

- Barcode reader …reads (thickness of pairs of) lines (and turns them into a code)/scans code with laser
- Magnetic Stripe …on back of card, containing member no. magnetically
- Keyboard/manual input …in case automatic data entry fails, number can be typed in/keyboard

Describe two forms of output which could be produced by the system following the input of the membership number. [F451 Q5 Jan 2010 (2,2)]

- Sound/light …beep to signify that data has been accepted
- Image on screen …showing details of member and books borrowed

- Hardcopy output/printout …kept for later use, perhaps to provide evidence for updating other files

Define what is meant by a secondary storage device. [F451 Q1 Jan 2009 (1)]

- A peripheral/external unit which allows storage of data over a long period.

A sixth form student has a stand-alone desktop PC at home and also uses the computers at school. Name <u>three</u> different types of secondary storage device which she might have and give a use for each. [F451 Q1 Jan 2009 (2,2,2)]

- Hard drive …to store files/Operating System/software
- CD ROM drive/DVD ROM …to load software/use encyclopaedias
- CD RW/DVD RW …to backup or transport data
- Memory stick …to move data between school and home

1.2 Describe the purpose of input devices, storage devices and output devices

The purpose of an input device is to bring data into a computer system for processing. An example might include using a digital camera to input images for later processing by a graphics package before being included in a web page or a document. The purpose of an output device is to take the processed data and output it in a form suitable for us to make use of. An example might be a printed document or the sound of the latest hit single played through a set of speakers. Storage devices save user data, programs and applications for later use.

Input devices are not restricted to keyboards and mice. An input device might for example consist of a sensor, perhaps a pressure sensor to determine when someone or something has stood on a pressure sensitive mat, or a temperature sensor or thermistor to determine the temperature of a room. In such situations a complementary output device might very well consist of an actuator or motor which opens a door in the first instance or turns on a pump in the second.

A sixth form student uses different forms of secondary storage media with her computer system. For each of the following secondary storage media, state what the student may use it for. In each case identify a characteristic of the medium which makes it suitable for the use. Hard disk, DVD ROM and Solid state pen drive. [F451 Q7 Jan 2011 (2,2,2)]

Hard disk drive :

- Store software/OS/data files ... large capacity/fast access to data

DVD ROM :

- Import of software/Encyclopaedias ... cannot be written to/information cannot be changed

Solid state pen drive :

- Transport work to and from school/make back ups ... small/light/large capacity/portable/usable on any machine/robust

A central heating system is used to control the heating in a house. State an automatic input device which would be used with this system, explaining why it is necessary. State an automatic output device which would be used with this system, explaining why it is necessary. [F451 Q1 Jun 2011 (2,2)]

- Temperature sensor/thermistor/thermostat ... to give the computer/processor information about the temperature of the room
- Actuator/heater ... used to turn heater on/used to heat up room/used to turn pump on

State two reasons why it is necessary to have at least one storage device in addition to the computers memory in a computer system. [F451 Q1 Specimen Questions (2)]

- Contents of memory lost when power switched off
- Size of memory not sufficient to store all the software/data required
- Need to import/export files

A client file at a firm of solicitors requires pictures to be stored to identify the clients. Describe two methods of capturing the pictures for the system. [F451 Q3 Jan 2010 (2,2)]

- Scanner to input picture already in hard copy ... pixels scanned/reflected light measured
- Electronic camera to take picture ... lens focuses image onto matrix of receptors/transferred via cable/memory card/USB to computer

1.3 DESCRIBE THE DIFFERENT ROLES AND FUNCTIONS OF SYSTEMS SOFTWARE AND APPLICATIONS PACKAGES

Systems software controls the hardware, provides a user interface, manages memory, provides a platform for applications and provides services such as printing and file handling. Application packages are programs that allow the user to do something useful, such as a word processor or internet browser.

Describe the difference between systems software and applications software. [F451 Q1 Specimen Questions (2)]

- Systems software controls the hardware/makes the system useable by the operator
- Applications software allows the user to carry out a useful task (which would need to be carried out even if computers did not exist)

A student will use both systems software and applications software. State the purpose of each of these. [F451 Q1 Jan 2011 (2)]

- System software ... controls the hardware of the computers/gives a platform to run other software/controls operation of computer system/provides communications
- Applications software ... makes the hardware/allows the user to, do something useful/carries out a task (which would have had to be done without a computer)

A business exists which specialises in supplying laptop computers to students. The business maintains a large customer base and carries out full servicing on the laptops. It carries a full stock of all the different types available. The managing director, Karen, decides to computerise the administration of the business. State three different types of applications software which Karen may decide are necessary for running the business, saying what they would be used for. [F451 Q8 Specimen Questions (2,2,2)]

- Stock control ... to ensure there is always stock available of different types
- Order processing ... to ensure that orders are completed and that new stock arrives
- Payroll ... to control the pay and tax of employees
- Word processor ... to write letters to customers
- Spreadsheet ... to produce accounts of the business
- Desk Top Publishing ... production of an instruction manual
- Presentation software ... to produce presentations to be used with groups
- Web authoring ... to produce a company website
- Database ... to store customer records

Software

2.1 DESCRIBE THE STAGES OF THE SYSTEMS LIFE CYCLE

The systems life cycle describes the various stages that are gone through in analysing, designing and implementing a new computer system. The commonly agreed definition of these stages are feasibility study, analysis, design, implementation, testing, installation and maintenance. Whereas each stage feeds into subsequent stages, looping of stages will inevitably occur. For example, evaluation might necessitate changes to the design which which are then fed back through development, installation, further testing and subsequently further evaluation.

A systems analyst has been in charge of creating an automated production line for a factory. The analyst followed the stages of the systems life cycle. Describe the purpose of three of the stages of the systems life cycle which the analyst must complete before the software can be written. [F451 Q6 Jun 2011 (2,2,2)]

- Definition of problem ...if problem not defined accurately then the wrong problem will be solved/client will not be happy despite the analyst solving the problem
- Feasibility study...decision made as to whether the problem can be solved/Parameters like budget and work force considered
- Information collection ...example of information collection method
- Analysis of information collected ...formulation of requirements specification/creates an understanding of problem and present solutions
- Design of solution ...design specification created / Data structures planned / interface planned / diagrams used to explain new solution

2.2 Explain the importance of defining a problem accurately

A poorly defined problem will lead to a poor solution, unhappy customers who don't get what they want and unhappy developers who probably won't get paid. Problems need to be defined and understood clearly and correctly if there is to be any chance of producing a correct and appropriate solution. Misunderstandings can quickly arise between the client and the developer because whilst the client understands his or her business, the client is unlikely to understand technology as well as the developer who in turn is unlikely to understand the client's business.

A dairy company collects milk from farms and processes it before supplying dairy products to shops. It is taking over another business which will increase its size significantly. The decision is made to employ a systems analyst to produce a new computer system to help run the business. Explain why the problem must be defined accurately before the analyst starts work. [F451 Q5 Jan 2009 (3)]

- The client does not understand the potential of computer systems
- The analyst does not understand the dairy industry
- The two must pool their information in order to ensure the right problem is solved
- The analyst may produce a solution which does not satisfy the client

A systems analyst has been asked to produce a piece of software for a manager in an organisation. Explain the importance of accurately defining the problem to be solved and state what each of the analyst and the manager are able to contribute to the problem definition. [F451 Q2 Jan 2011 (4)]

- The two people involved will have very different ideas of the problem / Necessary that they solve problem which they agree on ... or manager will be unhappy/software will be useless ... and the analyst will not be paid.
- Analyst is expert in use of computers
- Manager is expert in area of problem

2.3 Describe the function and purpose of a feasibility study

A feasibility study should ideally precede any extensive work on a project and is intended to determine whether the problem under consideration is actually worth undertaking. This determination can be assessed under a number of headings. Firstly, it is important to consider whether the problem is technically feasible. I.e. can the problem be solved, can software be written or hardware designed to actually solve the problem. Secondly, if the problem can be solved, can it be done in an acceptable time frame. Thirdly, is it legally feasible. For example, does the solution infringe any patents or perhaps involve criminal activity. Fourthly, is it socially feasible, for example are the social consequences of the solution such that an unacceptably large number of people are likely to lose their employment because of it. Finally, is it economically and financially feasible, i.e. can the problem be solved at an acceptable price.

A system analyst is employed to investigate the introduction of a new computer system to an organisation by carrying out a feasibility study. Describe <u>three</u> factors which the analyst should consider about the proposed system. [F451 Q4 Jun 2009 (2,2,2)]

- Technical feasibility ... can hardware/software be found to implement the solution?
- Economic feasibility ... is the proposed solution possible within budget/economic to run?
- Social feasibility ... is the effect on the humans involved too extreme to be allowed/Environmentally sound?
- Skill level required/operational ... is there enough skill in the workforce?
- What is the expected effect on the customer? ... if the customer is not impressed then there may not be a point
- Legal ... can the problem be solved within the law?
- Time ... Is the time scale acceptable?

A firm of solicitors has been using a computer system which keeps records of its clients and other information necessary for the running of the business. It has been decided to replace the system with a more up-to-date one. A systems analyst has been appointed to supervise the replacement. The systems analyst will need to carry out a feasibility study. Describe the function and purpose of a feasibility study. [F451 Q3 Jan 2010 (5)]

- Technically feasible?
- Economically feasible?
- Is the workforce capable of running new system?
- Consideration of budget
- Socially feasible?
- Is the proposed system legal?
- Is the proposed system possible ... in given time period?
- Purpose is to carry out initial enquiries ... to see if there are any reasons why new system may not be acceptable ... before starting to produce it
- Plan may be revised if study highlights problems

2.4   Explain the importance of determining the information requirements of a system and describe different methods of fact finding

Determining the information requirements of a problem is essential to providing an acceptable working solution.

Fact finding includes *questionnaires*, the advantages of which are that questionnaires can target quickly a large number of potential users, are relatively simple to create and can cover a variety of topics simultaneously. The disadvantages are that many people don't bother to fill them in, they have a restricted set of questions and these are usually fairly limited in scope.

Observation has the advantage in that it possible to see what actually happens rather than what one is told, but people often behave differently when they are being observed and it can take a long time.

Structured interviews are useful in determining details of the problem. If they are one on one they can be very illuminating, but can take a long time. If they are in the form of group meetings, a lot of data can be gathered quickly, but one or two members can easily dominate discussions.

Documents can be collected and analysed. If well maintained, documentation can be invaluable in determining how the system currently operates, but documentation may be incorrect and not up to date thus not accurately reflecting the current state of the system.

A systems analyst has been employed to update a computer system in a business. State three ways to collect information, giving an advantage and a disadvantage of each. [F451 Q2 Specimen Questions (3,3,3)]

Interviews:

- Allow departure from prepared script/allows interviewee to elaborate on points/makes clients believe they are fully involved; time consuming/only gives the view of one person/biased views can be anonymous/cost effective

Questionnaires:

- Allow a large number to have their say in a short time/allows all to feel involved; very rigid structure/does not allow individual points/person filling it in may feel rail roaded/poor return

Observation of current system:

- See system warts and all/see system with new eyes/see information workers may feel not important; workers may not act naturally/may not see abnormal procedures/business may be cyclical

Collection of documentation:

- Gives clear indication of inputs and outputs necessary/shows what workers and management find acceptable; present documentation may not be effective/may be difficult to understand without more information

Explain why a systems analyst needs to identify the information requirements of a system, AND describe the different methods of fact finding that may be used.
[F451 Q4 Jun 2010 (8)]

The examiners will expect the answer to include the following points …

- Need to ensure analyst understands the organisation requirements or the system produced may not meet requirements
- Need to ensure correct hardware and software
- Interview; one to one situation can change course of questions, can also hold one on one with the client
- Questionnaire; many have their views considered, can be time saving if there is a large workforce
- Observation; can see process in action, but employees may not act as they would because being observed
- Meeting; can get views from many people at once, but may be taken over by one or two people
- Document collection/indicates what data is actually collected.

2.5 DESCRIBE WHAT IS INVOLVED WHEN ANALYSING THE REQUIREMENTS OF A SYSTEM, EXPLAINING THE NATURE OF THE REQUIREMENTS SPECIFICATION AND ITS CONTENT

The requirements specification pulls together all information gathered in the analysis stage. It often forms the basis of the contract between customer and developer. It provides a complete specification of the problem including a (usually very long) list of all of the features that the solution must provide and all conditions under which the solution will work. Requirements specifications often include details on development milestones which normally trigger payments to the developer. If, at the end of the project, there is disagreement over whether the system actually does what it was supposed to do, the requirements specification is the final arbiter. It is essential that the requirements specification is properly detailed to ensure that nothing is left out or is ambiguous. It will include include details on current data structures, inputs and outputs, usually in the form of detailed diagrams and printouts, hardware and software requirements. It will often detail deficiencies with the current system.

State THREE items of content in the requirements specification of a system. [F451 Q4 Jun 2010 (3)]

- Input requirements
- Output requirements
- Processing requirements
- Clients agreement to requirements
- Hardware
- Software

2.6   DESCRIBE A DESIGN SPECIFICATION

The design stage follows directly from the analysis. The design specification describes in excruciating detail exactly how the new system is going to work. It will include detailed mock-ups of all data input and output forms, report structures, diagrams of the overall system, algorithms, data dictionaries, data life history diagrams, entity relationship diagrams flowcharts and anything else that might prove relevant. The design specification should be detailed enough so that any competent programmer could pick it up and create the new system.

State THREE items of content in the design specification of a system. [F451 Q4 Jun 2010 (3)]

- Input design
- Output design/choice of interface
- Data structure (design)
- Diagram of overall system
- Processing necessary/algorithms/flowcharts
- System flow charts
- Data flow diagrams
- Entity Relationship Diagrams
- Sitemaps

2.7   Explain the importance of evaluating the system, and how to identify the criteria used for evaluation

Any new system has to be evaluated to ensure that it meets all of the design and re-quirement specification objectives, thus confirming that it works as intended.

Explain the importance of evaluating a system and the criteria that should be used in the evaluation. [F451 Q6 Jun 2011 (4)]

- Client must evaluate system to ensure that the requirements have been met
- Analyst must evaluate system to provide evidence that they should be paid
- The criteria should be the agreed set of objectives of the system
- This will be done by the rigorous testing of the system ... including normal and abnormal data, i.e. functional testing ... and using the end user as a tester/acceptance testing

2.8   Explain the content and importance of different types of documentation at different stages in the system life cycle

Documentation on the new system will have been produced throughout the design process. Users will need their own documentation which will provide a complete blow by blow account of how to use the new system, how to handle errors, how to back up the system, how to get further help and so on. The maintenance program-mers will need a technical manual detailing all of the data structures, algorithms, flowcharts, data flow diagrams, entity relationship diagrams and code used in the new system.

The completed solution includes user and technical manuals. State the purpose of each manual. [F451 Q2 Specimen Questions (2)]

- *User manual:* Gives instructions to software users to allow them to successfully produce the desired results/explain error messages/what the user has done wrong.
- *Technical manual:* Describes how the system works

The analyst produces user and technical documentation for a new system. State three items which would be contained in the user documentation. [F451 Q3 Jan 2010 (3)]

- Input/Output procedures
- Using processing tools/how to operate the system

- Backing up and archiving (procedures)
- File searching/maintenance of files
- Error messages/trouble shooting
- FAQ
- Help available
- Required hardware specifications/system set up procedure
- Glossary
- Index/contents

Describe two kinds of diagram which may be in the technical documentation.
[F451 Q3 Jan 2010 (4)]

- DFD ... showing flow of data through system
- System flow chart ... showing how parts of system interrelate
- Flowchart ... showing the operations involved/the algorithm
- ERD ... shows how data tables relate to each other

2.9 Explain the importance of system testing and installation planning

The new system will need extensive testing to ensure that all aspects of the system are working as planned. Test plans are created during the design process and these will be followed to ensure that everything is working. System installation can be done in a number of ways.

Direct changeover: the old system is shut down and the new system turned on - usually only used if there are no other choices since new systems rarely work first time out.

Parallel changeover: the new system is installed alongside the old system. Both systems run together on the normal data. When the new system is clearly working, the old system can be turned off.

Pilot changeover: if possible the new system is installed in one location where it will run, often for many months before it is rolled out in other locations. Alternatively, the new system is operated alongside the old system but with a subset of the data.

Phased changeover: some tasks previously performed by the old system are replaced with the new system. As confidence grows in the new system more and more tasks are undertaken by the new system until eventually the old system can be completely replaced.

When software has been completed, its installation will need to be planned. Describe two tasks which an analyst needs to plan as part of the installation strategy. [F451 Q2 Jan 2011 (2,2)]

- Method of implementation/mention of one or more of: parallel/pilot/phased/direct
- Training program must be devised/materials written
- Files must be created/need to produce files/adapt or reformat present ones
- Hardware must be bought/installed/commissioned
- System must be tested/with real data files/by users
- Post monitoring for errors/provide technical documentation

2.10 EXPLAIN THE PURPOSE OF MAINTAINING THE SYSTEM, AND EXPLAIN THE NEED FOR SYSTEM REVIEW AND REASSESSMENT

All systems need maintenance.

Corrective: the new system may suffer from bugs which need to be fixed.

Perfective: the management may wish to improve or enhance the system with new or modified features.

Adaptive: regulations may change and the new system may need to be modified in line with new guidelines. All software has a limited lifespan since hardware is constantly improving, things that were initially impossible now become possible, storage requirements that may have being considered too large may be now easily achievable. Companies change as they grow and new requirements require new systems.

Describe two types of maintenance which may need to be carried out on any finished system. [F451 Q6 Jun 2011 (2,2)]

- Corrective ... errors will be found in original software/only come to light in normal use/missed by testing/must be corrected to make software usable
- Adaptive ... one of the parameters used to set up system has changed/e.g. the VAT rate changes/the software must be altered to reflect the change
- Perfective ... during use it is found that one element of the system is not performing as well as it could/software is altered to improve performance

2.11 DESCRIBE PROTOTYPING TO DEMONSTRATE HOW A SOLUTION WILL APPEAR

Prototyping is the creation of a working model of a system to show its essential features. Feedback from the customer will result in a new, improved prototype which will be subject to further feedback and eventually over time, as more and more features of the prototype are included, the final solution will emerge. This is the RAD (Rapid Application Development) approach.

Describe how prototyping can be used by the analyst as part of the design process. [F451 Q2 Jan 2011 (4)]

- (Simple version of program to) illustrate a feature of the software
- Normally used to illustrate input and output screens
- The screens are dummies in that they elicit no action
- Used to show manager the way system will look/ allows issues to be spotted
- Allow manager to be part of the design process/to give feedback/evaluate
- Used to research new ideas
- Used to refine prototype
- May include a story board showing linking of screens

2.12 DESCRIBE THE SPIRAL AND WATERFALL MODELS OF THE SYSTEMS LIFE CYCLE

The spiral is often indistinguishable from the RAD approach in that prototypes are built, amended and the process repeated until one eventually 'spirals in' to the final solution. The waterfall model is the traditional Feasibility, Analysis Design, etc. approach.

An analyst decides to use the spiral model of the systems life cycle. Describe the spiral model. [F451 Q4 Jun 2009 (2)]

- Analyst begins by collecting data followed by each of the other stages leading to . . . evaluation, which will lead to . . . a return to data collection to modify the results
- Important point is that the different stages are refined each time the spiral is worked through
- The above points, shown in diagrammatic form, are acceptable

An analyst uses the waterfall model of the systems life cycle. Describe the waterfall model. [F451 Q6 Jun 2011 (3)]

- Idea of passing from one stage to the next in order
- Each stage in the life cycle feeds information to the next stage
- At each stage it may be necessary to return to one or more previous stages . . . either to collect more information/data or to check on data that has been collected
- After returning, all the intervening steps must be revisited

The examiners will often cover a wide range of the specification in a single extended question. The following example illustrates the type of question you might expect to find.

A dairy company collects milk from farms and processes it before supplying dairy products to shops. It is taking over another business which will increase its size significantly. The decision is made to employ a systems analyst to produce a new computer system to help run the business.

State why it is important to the client and to the analyst to evaluate the finished system. [F451 Q5 Jan 2009 (2)]

- Important to client because need to be sure it will perform as required/identifies areas where solution is lacking
- Important to analyst because it determines the end of the job/the analyst being paid

Identify three types of maintenance which will be necessary after the system is running, giving an example of why each is necessary. (2,2,2)

- Corrective ... to correct bugs found in software when being used
- Adaptive ... to alter software because of external need e.g. VAT paid on dairy produce is changed to 10%
- Perfective ... to improve performance of software

Part of the system will involve a database containing information about the farms. The data stored will include

- **the name of the farmer**
- **the type of herd (a single letter between A-H, to describe the breed of cattle, followed by a 3 digit number to show the size of the herd)**
- **the last payment (in pounds and pence) made to the farmer**
- **the total volume of milk collected for the last three collections**

The first two items of data will be entered into the database by a keyboard operator. Name two different validation tests which would be carried out on the data entered and describe how they would be carried out. (2,2)

- Character check/type check ... letters of alphabet for name
- Length check ... herd type should be of length 4
- Format check ... herd type should be 1 character followed by 3 digits
- Presence check ... to ensure that a value has been entered
- Existence check ... farmers name is already in file

The information about payments is imported to the database from another type of software. State the type of software which would be used to calculate the payments. (1)

- Accounting package or spreadsheet

The final piece of data is the result of adding up the volumes from the last three collections. These values are stored as 12 bit binary numbers. Do the following addition of three days of collections. Show your working.
010010010010 + 001110000010 + 011000110001 (3)

0	1	0	0	1	0	0	1	0	0	1	0
0	0	1	1	1	0	0	0	0	0	1	0
0	1	1	0	0	0	1	1	0	0	0	1
1	1	1	0	0	1	0	0	0	1	0	1
1	1	1	1		1				1		

Some of the farmers whose data is to be stored on the database are worried about allowing the data to be stored. Discuss the reasons why the farmers may be worried and the measures which the dairy company can take to alleviate their fears. (8)

To get the full quota of marks on extended questions it is sensible to firstly spend a little time drawing up a list of bullet points covering the areas specified in the question. (Extended questions are questions where you are told that the quality of your written communication will be assessed in your answer to the question and are often worth 8 marks). For example, in this question you need to discuss *both* why the farmers may be worried and *also* what measures can be taken by the dairy company to alleviate their fears. Good answers will use technical terms correctly and appropriately. In this particular example the examiners will be looking for coverage of the following points.

Reasons/Concerns/Worries:

- Privacy of their personal details
- Commercially sensitive data about the farm
- Being hacked into by outsiders
- Being sold on by company or employees
- Errors in data being stored leading to ...compounded errors when data used in calculations
- Farmers from new area do not have experience of working with company

Measures:

- Allow access to data by farmers in order to ...check accuracy
- Limit access to small number of named personnel
- Abide by data protection legislation
- Take measures such as firewalls to stop hacking
- Use satisfied farmers to placate worries among new customers

2.13   IDENTIFY THE FEATURES OF COMMON APPLICATIONS FOUND IN BUSINESS, COMMERCIAL AND INDUSTRIAL APPLICATIONS

Stock control systems manage product inventory, i.e. how many tins of baked beans do we have in stock, if less than a pre-agreed stocking level, then re-order. All businesses have administrative departments that look after order processing (i.e. managing customer orders, by selling one's own products (sales order processing) and (invariably) buying other companies' products, managing the payroll, i.e paying the employees. Most businesses need a sales force, a marketing department and some such as architects or engineering firms will use Computer Aided Design (CAD) software to design products that are later manufactured, often using Computer Aided Manufacturing (CAM) systems.

The entire production process of a factory, including rolling sheet metal, is computerised. The process is controlled from a central control room which is operated by a single operator. Describe the different forms of output that would be used to present information to the operator. [F451 Q8 Jan 2011 (6)]

- Graphs ...to show trends/thickness of sheet against time
- Interactive presentations ...(eg touch screen) to allow report and action (increase or decrease of pressure on rollers)
- Sound/light ...to present alarm signals/eg sheet too thick despite repeated rolling
- Text using flash/reverse colour/different colours/position on screen ...methods of giving a second type of information apart from what is actually stated
- Video/Images ...to show operator production line/eg see reason for blockage
- Hard copy/printout ...for future reference/research

Explain why the quality of the interface design is important in applications like this. (6)

- Large amount of information ...only one operator
- Operator might miss seeing info
- Info must be ordered
- Danger of information overload ...needs to be prioritised

- Some information is crucial, like line blockage ... must be presented in way that has immediate impact
- Use of colour must be consistent
- Use of sound must be minimal otherwise it will be ignored
- Must consider operator/is the operator colour blind/deaf/capable?

2.14 IDENTIFY AND JUSTIFY GENERIC APPLICATIONS SOFTWARE FOR PARTICULAR APPLICATION AREAS

Generic applications are applications which can perform a number of useful functions. For example a word processor can be used to write documents, create fliers, write books and generally do many of the things that people want to do with the printed word. Generic applications are usually bought 'off the shelf' for not a great deal of money. They are tried and testing, have excellent user support and are usually very well documented, thus relatively straightforward to learn.

The marketing department is responsible for advertising the products produced by a factory. State two types of generic applications software that the marketing department would use and describe what they would be used for. [F451 Q8 Jan 2011 (2,2)]

- DTP ... used for producing brochures/leaflets/flyers
- Drawing package ... to produce adverts/leaflets/flyers
- Graphics ... to create images
- Digital editor ... to edit sound/video for presentation
- Word Processor ... to produce letters/emails
- Presentation software ... used for producing multi media presentation for an audience
- Communications software ... used for sending mass emails
- Web authoring software ... used for maintaining company website

The sales department stores customer records and is responsible for communications with customers. State two types of generic applications software that the sales department would use and describe what they would be used for. [F451 Q8 Jan 2011 (2,2)]

- Database ... to store files of customers and sales
- Word processor ... to write to customers/mail merge to send material to specific types of customer
- Communications software ... to send emails to customers
- Spreadsheets ... to keep records of sales/calculate invoices

A business exists which specialises in supplying laptop computers to students. The business maintains a large customer base and carries out full servicing on the laptops. It carries a full stock of all the different types available. The managing director, Karen, decides to computerise the administration of the business. State three different types of applications software which Karen may decide are necessary for running the business, saying what they would be used for. [F451 Q8 Specimen Questions (2,2,2)]

- Stock control ... to ensure there is always stock available of different types
- Order processing ... to ensure that orders are completed and that new stock arrives
- Payroll ... to control the pay and tax of employees
- Word processor ... to send letters to customers
- Spreadsheet ... to produce accounts of the business
- Desk Top Publishing ... for production of an instruction manual
- Presentation software ... to produce presentations to be used with groups
- Web authoring ... to produce a company website
- Database ... to store customer records

2.15   IDENTIFY AND JUSTIFY APPLICATION AREAS FOR WHICH CUSTOM-WRITTEN APPLICATIONS SOFTWARE IS APPROPRIATE

Some areas such as medical or mobile platforms require custom written software. These products are created from scratch by experienced developers specifically to solve a particular problem for the customer and are often very expensive, poorly documented with little or no customer support. Well written custom software can however produce solutions that generic software cannot.

Part of a factory production line takes blocks of metal as input and passes them between rollers to flatten them into sheets. The process is computer controlled in order to produce sheets of the correct size and thickness. Explain why custom-written software is used to control the process rather than generic applications software. [F451 Q8 Jan 2011 (2)]

- Process is unique/a one-off
- Generic software will not exist (to do just this)
- The generic control software will have many unused features/ bespoke written specifically for this purpose
- Custom-written can be written to allow ease of changes to production

2.16 Describe the characteristics of knowledge-based systems

Knowledge based systems have rules, facts, an inference engine and a user interface used to query the system. Often called an 'expert' system, the system uses an inference engine to analyse the facts and rules to produce answers to user questions entered via the user interface. Typical examples include diagnostic systems using in car testing or medicine.

Many customers carry a store loyalty card which is scanned at the checkout. The data collected is stored in the knowledge-base of a knowledge based (expert) system. State <u>three</u> other parts which will make up the knowledge based system and say why each part is necessary. [F451 Q1 Jun 2009 (2,2,2)]

- Rule base ... contains all the rules that can be applied to the knowledge/data
- Inference engine ... software which uses the rules in the rule base and searches through the knowledge base
- HCI ... allows for data or queries to be input and results to be output

One part of a factory making sheet metal is the foundry. It is here that metals are melted and then mixed in the right proportions and by the right methods to produce suitable alloys. These alloys can then be used in the factory. A knowledge based system (expert system) is used to provide information to ensure that the production of the alloys is successful. Describe how a knowledge based system is set up. [F451 Q8 Jan 2011 (4)]

- Experts in the field are interviewed, information is collected from many sources
- This information is used to create a knowledge base
- The rules used to interrogate the knowledge base are collected in the rules base
- The rules are used to interrogate the knowledge base using a set of algorithms stored in the inference engine
- An HCI is set up to provide communication outside the knowledge-based system

2.17 Describe the purpose of operating systems

Operating systems control the hardware, provide a user interface and services for application programs. They also manage memory usage, provide utility programs and file handling facilities. They provide the software platform on which application programs run.

In the following question and in questions that use the word describe, the examiners are looking for a description and then an expansion as to why or how the object in question is useful or important.

Describe four purposes of operating systems. [F451 Q2 Jun 2010 (2,2,2,2)]

- Used to control the hardware of the system/resource management ...through software like hardware drivers/system software
- Used to provide a platform on which applications can run ...deals with issues that the software may have with e.g. storage of files
- Provides a user interface with operator ...to allow communication between user & hardware
- Handles communications ...using rules/protocols to govern the communication
- Handles translation of code ...e.g. compiler/interpreter
- Has many utility programs ...used to carry out housekeeping on system/example
- Different types/mention of type ...for different circumstances/any sensible example

2.18 DESCRIBE THE CHARACTERISTICS OF DIFFERENT TYPES OF OPERATING SYSTEMS AND THEIR USES

Batch systems take a large amount of identically formatted data and process it at a suitable time, often late at night or on the weekend where user involvement is not required. A typical example might be processing the payroll for employees in a business.

A *real-time* system is one in which processing is done fast enough so that any input is processed sufficiently quickly to affect subsequent input. An example might include a flight booking system. Booking a seat means that it cannot be subsequently booked by anyone else, anywhere in the world. A second example might be a computer game where the player's input affects any subsequent output.

A *single-user* operating system will only allow a single user to use the computer at any one time.

A *multi-user* operating system can handle (potentially) many users simultaneously.

A *multi-tasking* operating system allows any user to run many tasks (seemingly) simultaneously.

A *multi-user, multi-tasking* operating system will allow many users to each run (potentially) many tasks (apparently) simultaneously.

Workers in a factory each have a swipe card which contains their identification number. This card is swiped through a reader when they arrive at work in the morning and again when they leave at night. The workers are paid on Friday each week. Explain why a batch operating system is used to produce the payroll. [F451 Q1 Jan 2010 (5)]

- Inputs are stored
- Because only useful when full week of values collected
- Payroll run on Thursday night/once a week/all at the same time
- No need for human to be present
- Run in computer downtime/when workers have gone home
- No need for instant response to inputs
- All processing is similar/data is of similar type
- Large amount of data

State an application of a computer system which requires a real-time operating system, justifying your choice. [F451 Q1 Jan 2010 (2)]

- Airline booking system …because it is important that the system is updated before the next input so no double booking
- Computer game …because it is important that the system is updated before the next input to avoid any game lag

The operating system of a stand-alone personal computer can usually be described as a single-user, multi-tasking operating system. Describe what is meant by an operating system. [F451 Q4 Jan 2009 (2)]

- A set of software/programs …designed to manage the hardware of the system.

Describe a single-user operating system. (3)

- Allows one user …at a time to use the system
- Allocates each user with rights
- Keeps the user files separate

Describe a multi-tasking operating system. (3)

- Allows more than one task/software to run (apparently) simultaneously
- Use of separate windows for each task
- Each is given an amount of processor time before …going on to next
- E.g. playing music while typing essay

Describe each of the following types of operating system and give an example of where each could be used: multi-tasking, multi-user. [F451 Q9 Jun 2011 (4,4])

Multi-tasking

- Allows more than one task/program to be open at a time ... each apparently runs at the same time
- Processor is so fast that it seems as though the tasks are done simultaneously
- Round robin system with each task allowed a small amount of time
- User can switch between programs
- Different programs available in different windows
- *Use:* e.g. Single user/student able to listen to music while using a spreadsheet/single machine operating system

Multi-user

- One computer with many terminals/more than one user at a time
- Each terminal given time slice ... in turn
- Each time slice very small (roughly 1/100 of a second)
- Use of flags
- Use of priorities/privileges
- Data is separated/ security provision essential/user rights
- *Use:* e.g. Supermarket checkout system/online gaming/mainframe serving many terminals

2.19 DESCRIBE A RANGE OF APPLICATIONS REQUIRING BATCH PROCESSING, AND APPLICATIONS IN WHICH A RAPID RESPONSE IS REQUIRED

Batch processing: is characterised by situations in which a large volume of data needs to be processed in a similar fashion but where human intervention is not required and often the processing can take place outside of normal working hours. Examples will include but are not limited to payroll processing, production of bank statements and utility bill creation.

Real-time: systems are systems which react quickly enough to influence behaviour in the real world. Examples include but are not limited to games, flight simulators, air-traffic systems and flight bookings.

2.20   Identify and describe the purpose of different types of user interface

Forms are a form of user interface 'in which computer outputs separate *prompt* and response fields for a number of inputs'[1]. They often include drop down boxes, text fields, radio buttons and check boxes and are used to ensure that appropriate data is collected properly and that nothing is missed. There is usually validation of user input. They are excellent for structured data input.

Menus lead to further menus that can lead to further menus each time 'drilling down' until the target information is available. They are excellent for naive computer users or in situations where a limited number of options are available. They are quick, easy to use and intuitive.

GUIs use windows, icons, menus and pointers to provide a visually appealing interface. They are effective for relatively experienced users. They have extensive functionally and are capable of running an unlimited range of applications.

Natural language interfaces are intuitive since speech is human's most intuitive mode of operation. They are appropriate for for (almost) anyone. They are however poor in noisy environments, not good with accents and need training by the user.

Command line interfaces require the user to write (usually) single lines of commands for the computer to carry out. The user has to know what commands are available and appropriate for what he or she wishes to do. This interface is very powerful in the hands of the experienced user especially when the commands are combined into short programs, but can be frustrating for those who do not know what commands are available.

(b) The office staff at a sales company will use a GUI interface, while the people who take orders over the telephone will use a form-based interface. Describe each of these interfaces. [F451 Q8 Specimen Questions (2,2)]

(i) GUI

- Use of icons
- Use of windows or frames
- Use of pointers and menus

---

[1]A glossary of computing terms, British Computing Socity

Form-based

- Computer outputs prompts
- User responds
- Data proscribed and ordered

(ii) Explain why a forms interface is appropriate for use by workers taking orders over the telephone. (3)

- Prompts questions to ask customers
- Ensures no necessary information is missed
- Provides list of possible choices to some questions
- Allows for simplified validation process

For each of the following user interfaces, give an example of an application of its use, the hardware which would be used with the interface in your application and describe why it is suitable for the application. [F451 Q7 Jun 2010 (4,4)]

(i) Menu based interface

- E.g. tourist information system
- E.g. touch screen/pointing device
- Simple to use
- Limited choices
- Suitable for environment

(ii) Natural language interface

- E.g. Expert systems
- E.g. Keyboard or microphone
- Allows user to use human syntax
- Very complex systems therefore simplification of query is useful
- User may find use of a natural syntax easier, so can focus on application

Visitors to a small business use a menu based interface in the reception area. Describe a menu based interface. [F451 Q7 Jan 2009 (3)]

- List of choices on screen
- Choice made by user leading to ... further menus
- Can use touch screen
- Back/home options on each screen

Explain why this interface is offered to visitors, rather than a GUI. (3)

- Limit on choices valuable for people with little knowledge to help them decide

- Restricts users to those areas of system which the company is happy for them to visit
- Use of touch screen limits damage /vandalism
- Easy to use/intuitive/GUI more difficult to use
- May be computer illiterate

2.21   Discuss the importance of good interface design

It is important that computer interfaces are relevant and appropriate to the user. Various factors need to be considered when designing a new interface. For example, are the expected users likely to be experienced or inexperienced? Interfaces for inexperienced users will need to be simpler and more intuitive that that for experienced users. What is the purpose of the interface and what is the environment in which the interface will be used? If, as in the next question, the interface will be used in a manufacturing setting, the environment is likely to be noisy, it is quite likely to be dirty, information will need to be conveyed to the operators quickly and unambiguously and they are unlikely to be experienced computer users.

A manufacturing company uses computers for both the manufacturing process and the tasks carried out in the offices. The computerised manufacturing process is controlled by a single operator. State <u>three</u> factors which should have been considered when designing the output interface for the operator. Give a reason for each. [F451 Q7 Jun 2009 (2,2,2)]

- Form of output ... e.g. sound may be inappropriate/inaccurate on a noisy factory floor
- Volume of data ... e.g. operator must not be subjected to information overload as this may lead to omissions
- Colours used ... e.g. must be enough contrast to make it readable/sensible use of colours like red for danger
- Limited use of effects like reverse video ... the more they are used, the less the impact
- Use of diagrams ... easy to relate data to position without need for extra information.
- Experience of operator ... e.g. CLI not suitable for inexperienced operator
- Short/Long term memory ... operator must not be expected to remember too much/for too long
- Operator disability ... to ensure that disability is not an issue
- Layout ... spread around screen/important information in top left of screen/no overload/font size
- Hardware choices ... suitability for both user and the application/environment to be used in

Answering questions of this nature requires you to draw upon your experience of, or your ability to imagine the use of computers in a variety of settings. In the next two questions you are asked to justify the use of a particular style of interface.

The interface on an interactive information kiosk used by holidaymakers is a menus interface. Explain why a menus interface was chosen for this application. [F451 Q3 Jun 2011 (3)]

- Simple to use/intuitive/requires no computing skill
- Leads user through a number of options/one menu leads to others
- Presents possibilities to user/acts as information system as well as search engine
- Does not allow user to enter other parts of system
- Navigation simple/allows return to previous screens easily if mistake is made/reduces number of errors
- Ideal for use with touchscreen

The interface used by workers in the tourist information office to book accommodation for holidaymakers is a forms interface. Explain why a forms interface was chosen for this application. (3)

- User needs to input information (so requires an interface which allows this)
- Input boxes force input to be made/guard against forgetting to give information
- Use of radio buttons/drop down lists
- Makes validation of information submitted easier
- Instructions for input are presented to user
- Processing simplified because information is standard

2.22 IDENTIFY AND DESCRIBE THE PURPOSE OF A RANGE OF UTILITIES

Utility programs are designed to perform some commonplace task, for example copying files from one medium to another, sorting or backing up data. Some of the more common ones are as follows.

Compression software reduces the size of data files. Compressing files is often essential for sending video and sound over the internet.

Hardware drivers add additional functionality to the operating system to allow the system to make use of a particular hardware device such as a new printer, camera, scanner or mobile phone.

Anti-virus software detects and destroys incoming computer viruses.

File handlers allow the user to create, delete, copy, move, open, close and view files.

State what is meant by utility software. [F451 Q9 Jun 2011 (1)]

- Housekeeping programs
- System program to perform a common task
- Programs to help the running of the software/hardware
- Anti-virus ... to protect system

A student uses a computer to produce coursework for a number of subjects. Explain how the student can use file handling utilities with the computer. (3)

- Storage of files on secondary storage
- Use of folders/directories/different file extensions
- Opening files/folders to retrieve data when required/use of shortcuts created on desktop
- Copying of files from one medium/place to another/to take into school/make backups
- Deletion of files from storage when coursework handed in/more recent version stored
- Security measures/access management

An author works from home using a computer system. She uses a number of pieces of utility software. State the purpose of each of these types of utility and describe how the author would use them in her work. [F451 Q6 Jan 2010 (3,3,3,3)]

Compression Software

- Reduces size of files
- When scripts are being sent electronically to publisher
- The compression means they are sent more quickly
- They are decompressed using a decompression algorithm at the destination

File handlers

- Manages data storage/organises data storage
- Allows files to be accessed
- Allows for deletion/sorting of files

Hardware drivers

- Contain the instructions to the OS for using a peripheral

- E.g. would be used when a new printer was bought ...in order to (install) communication (protocols) to OS/control of peripheral by OS
- To configure hardware

Backup utility

- Automatically ...makes copy of files
- To prevent loss of files
- Protects important work ...by ensuring it is stored on different hardware/at regular intervals
- Incremental backup made

3

Data: representation and structure

3.1 EXPRESS NUMBERS IN BINARY, BINARY-CODED DECIMAL, OCTAL AND HEXADECIMAL

Binary : a bit is 0 or 1. 4 bits = one nibble. 8 bits = one byte (two nibbles). 0 (denary) is represented in 8 bits as 00000000, 1 (denary) by 00000001, 2 by 00000010, and so on so that 128 (denary) = 10000000 and finally 255 is represented by 1111 1111 (if unsigned). Consequently, an unsigned byte can represent numbers from 0 through to 255.

You may have realised that each column in denary, for example 4,123 reading from right to left is increasing powers of 10. Similarly, each column in binary reading from right to left is increasing powers of 2. This gives us the following table which can be used to convert between binary and denary without too much effort.

2^7	2^6	2^5	2^4	2^3	2^2	2^1	2^0
128	64	32	16	8	4	2	1

So for, example if we put into the table the binary number 01100010

2^7	2^6	2^5	2^4	2^3	2^2	2^1	2^0
128	64	32	16	8	4	2	1
0	1	1	0	0	0	1	0

we can see that the number in denary is simply $2^6 + 2^5 + 2^1 = 64 + 32 + 2 = 98$

If we split a byte into two nibbles we can use hexadecimal to represent each nibble. So, by implication, a byte can be represented by two hex characters. Hex is base 16 and uses the numbers 0 - 9 and the letters A - F to represent the binary numbers 0000 to 1111. The full binary to hex to denary table is shown below.

0000	0	0	1000	8	8
0001	1	1	1001	9	9
0010	2	2	1010	A	10
0011	3	3	1011	B	11
0100	4	4	1100	C	12
0101	5	5	1101	D	13
0110	6	6	1110	E	14
0111	7	7	1111	F	15

To convert binary to hex simply split the byte into two nibbles, then write down the hex value of each nibble. So, for example the binary number 01100010 can be split into 0110 0010 which by reading the table you can see is the hexadecimal number 62. Similarly the binary number 10111010 i.e. 1011 1010 is the hexadecimal number BA.

Octal groups bits in threes so where the denary number 97 can be represented by the binary number 01100001 and in hex by 61, a 0 is added to the front of the number to give us 001100001 (i.e. nine bits) and the bits grouped in threes as 001 100 001 to give us the octal number 141.

Binary Coded Decimal (BCD) represents each digit of a denary number by its binary equivalent, so that 197 in denary would be written as 0001 1001 0111 in BCD.

Write the number 90 as a binary number in a single byte. [F451 Q4 Specimen Questions (2)]

- 90 = 64 + 16 + 8 + 2 = 01011010

Write the number 90 as a number in octal. (2)

- 01011010 = 001 011 010 = 132 in octal

Explain the relationship between the binary and octal representations of the number 90. (2)

- Groups of three binary bits (from the right)
- give octal digits when converted into decimal values.

Express the decimal number 95 in binary in a single 8-bit byte; in binary coded decimal in a single 8-bit byte; as a hexadecimal number. [F451 Q6 Jun 2009 (2,2,2)]

- 95 = 64 + 16 + 8 + 4 + 2 + 1 = 01011111
- 95 = 1001 0101 in binary coded decimal
- From the first part, 95 = 01011111 = 0101 1111 = 5F

Using your answers to the previous parts, explain how binary representation of numbers can be used to determine the hexadecimal value. (3)

- Arrange bits, in the binary value, in groups of 4 i.e. (0101, 1111)
- Each group of 4 is then written as its hexadecimal equivalent, (0101=5 , 1111=F) giving us 5F

3.2 DESCRIBE AND USE TWO'S COMPLEMENT AND SIGN AND MAGNITUDE TO REPRESENT NEGATIVE INTEGERS

We have a number of ways to represent negative binary numbers, two of which are considered below. In each case we use the most significant bit (i.e. the leftmost bit) to represent the minus sign. In what follows we are assuming that we are considering a single byte.

In *two's complement form* a 1 in that position can be thought of as representing the number -128 whereas the rest of the number remains positive. For example, 10010001 would represent $-128 + 16 + 1 = -111$.

In *sign and magnitude form* the most significant bit simply represents + (if it is 0) or - (if it is 1) The remainder of the byte is evaluated normally. For example, the same binary number (10010001) if encoded in sign and magnitude form would represent the number $-(16 + 1 = +17) = -17$.

1010111011 is an unsigned binary integer. State its denary value. [F451 Q4 Jan 2011 (1)]

- 699 (i.e. $512 + 128 + 32 + 16 + 8 + 2 + 1$)

1010111011 is a binary number in sign and magnitude form. State its denary value. (2)

- -187 (because … the most significant bit (the leftmost) is a 1 so the number is negative. The remaining bits represent $(128 + 32 + 16 + 8 + 2 + 1) = 187$ so the answer is -187.

1010111011 is a binary number in 2's complement form. State its denary value. (2)

- -325 (because … the most significant bit (the leftmost) is a 1 so the number is negative and since this is in two's complement form is worth -512. The remaining bits represent $(128 + 32 + 16 + 8 + 2 + 1) = 187$ so the final answer is $-512 + 187 = -325$.

Explain why sign and magnitude form is rarely used for computer arithmetic. (3)

- Two types of data in same byte / the msb is a sign ... must be treated differently from the rest of the byte
- Makes arithmetic algorithms very complex
- Extending from 1 byte to 2 or more bytes very difficult

Write the number −90 **as a twos complement binary number in a single byte.** [F451 Q4 Specimen Questions (1)]

- −90 = −128 + 32 + 4 + 2 = 10100110

Write the number −58 **as a twos complement binary number in a single byte.** (1)

- −58 = −128 + 64 + 4 + 2 = 11000110

Add the two answers obtained previously in a single byte. (2)

1	0	1	0	0	1	1	0
1	1	0	0	0	1	1	0
0	1	1	0	1	1	0	0
					1	1	

Explain the result. (2)

- Answer is +108 but it should be −148
- The largest magnitude negative number in a byte is −128 ... so the answer cannot be represented.

Using an 8 bit byte change −60 **into a twos complement binary number** [F451 Q5 Jun 2010 (2)]

- −60 = −128 + 64 + 4 = 11000100

Using 8 bit bytes describe how twos complement can be used by a computer to calculate the answer to 93 − 51. (4)

- 93 turned into 01011101
- 93 − 51 = 93 + (−51)
- (−51)= 11001101
- 100101010
- Ignore carry/00101010

3.3 PERFORM INTEGER BINARY ARITHMETIC, THAT IS ADDITION AND SUBTRACTION

In performing any binary arithmetic be sure to show the examiner your working. Marks are awarded for the working, in particular for showing how and when you carry 1s across from one column to the next.

10110010 and 00100110 are unsigned binary integers. Add together the binary numbers. (You must show your working.) [F451 Q4 Jan 2011 (2)]

1	0	1	1	0	0	1	0
0	0	1	0	0	1	1	0
1	1	0	1	1	0	0	0
	1			1	1		

Carry out the subtraction. (You must show your working) (2)

1	0	1	1^0	0^1	0^2	1	0
0	0	1	0	0	1	1	0
1	0	0	0	1	1	0	0

3.4 EXPLAIN THE USE OF CODE TO REPRESENT A CHARACTER SET

There is a need to represent text by appropriate binary codes. The most common are ASCII and in recent years, UNICODE.

ASCII is a 7-bit code that uses a single byte to represent a character. (the 8th most significant bit, originally used for error checking is now commonly used to provide a further 128 characters). In ASCII, the integer '0' is represented by 00110000, '1' by 00110001, 'A' by 01000001, 'B' by 01000010 and the characters '*' by 00101010 and '.' by 00101110 for example. One byte is too restrictive (it can only encode 256 different characters) for many of the world's languages so UNICODE which in its UTF-8 format uses four bytes, gives room for up to 4,294,967,296 different characters.

EBCDIC is an IBM mainframe character encoding system which uses one byte, but not the same encoding as ASCII. For example, the single character 'A' in EBCDIC is represented by the binary code 11000001.

Explain what is meant by the character set of a computer. [F451 Q8 Jan 2009 (2)]

- The symbols that the computer can recognise/use
- Each symbol is distinguishable from all others

- Normally determinable by reference to characters on keyboard
- E.g. ASCII/Unicode/EBCDIC

By referring to two examples of applications that need character sets of different sizes, explain how codes are used to represent character sets. (1,1,2)

- Word Processing / ATM Terminal
- Each required character is given a unique ... binary code
- The more characters required, the more bits in each code
- The number of bits to represent the code establishes the size of a byte
- E.g. ASCII or EBDIC using 8 bits per character, UNICODE using 16 bits
- This will give ASCII 256/128 characters
- ATM uses 10 digits + 6 command codes, 4 bits per character
- Number of characters will tend to be a power of 2
- Allows keys to have different characters

A car insurance firm collects data from its customers and stores it on a computer. The customer name is stored using the computers character set. Explain what is meant by the character set of a computer. [F451 Q4 Jun 2011 (2)]

- The symbols that may be represented/interpreted/understood by a computer
- Normally equates to the symbols on a keyboard/digits, letters etc.
- May include control characters

Explain the use of code to represent a character set. (2)

- Each character has a binary code/number ... which is unique
- Number of bits used for one character = 1 byte
- Example code/ ASCII/Unicode ... use 8 bits per character/16 bits per character
- Use of more bits for extended character set

3.5   DESCRIBE MANUAL AND AUTOMATIC METHODS OF GATHERING AND INPUTTING DATA INTO A SYSTEM

Good form design is essential. Forms need to be laid out so that data can be entered in a sensible, logical manner. Tab keys can be used to take users from item to item. Forms often reflect information held on paper in which case they need to be laid out in a similar manner. Fields on forms are often validated before submission. Normally, forms cannot be submitted until all of the necessary fields have been completed and validated. This ensures that all essential data has been entered.

Voice recognition is often used by telephone online services to enter credit card information and for simple yes/no responses to questions. They have military applications

- the most recent Eurofighter aeroplane uses pilot voice recognition systems for various cockpit functions. They can be of great benefit to disabled people who find it difficult or impossible to use a keyboard. Voice recognition software often needs to be trained by a user to recognise his or her particular voice and accent. Additionally, voice recognition in noisy environments is often very poor.

Bar codes are used to encode a sequence of digits in the form of varying width light and dark strips. They have a multitude of uses in all aspects of life from supermarkets to the health service. They are normally read using lasers and often form part of a stock control inventory system. Formerly one dimensional, two dimensional barcodes in the form of various geometric patterns are now in use.

Optical Mark Recognition (OMR) systems are used to determine whether a given mark is positioned at a particular position on a pre-designed form. Commonly used for multiple choice examination questions the OMR scanner shines a beam of light onto the form. The reflectivity of various parts of the form is used to determine whether that particular position represents a mark or not since dark areas reflect less light than lighter areas.

Optical Character Recognition (OCR) is the translation (usually) of a scanned electronic image of typed or handwritten text into an appropriate encoded form, usually ASCII or UNICODE that can then be read by a word processor. In its simplest form, the light and dark areas of the scanned image are compared to a library of known shapes and where matches occur the character is placed appropriately in a new document. OCR is used to encode all forms of written matter. Accuracy rates are extremely high in the case of well presented typed text where character recognition is relatively simple, but fall off dramatically in the case of handwritten text where characters can often be unrecognisable.

Magnetic Ink Character Recognition (MICR) is primarily used by the banking industry where characters are written onto cheques using magnetisable ink. These characters can be read by a device which magnetises and then identifies the character as it passes through the device. Error rates using such devices are very low.

Touch screens are often used where users are required to interact with a computer system, but only in pre-determined ways. Such examples would include information kiosks and factory control systems where it cannot be assumed that users are experienced in their use of computers and a menu based system is often used to take them through a list of options. More recently, touch screen technology has been deployed in smartphone devices such as the Apple iPhone and Google Android phones. In these instances, user interaction is very sophisticated and applications on the devices are able to use the touch sensitivity of the screen to create soft keyboards, swipe recognition and a variety of other techniques that give the user enormous flexibility in their use of the device.

Chip and pin systems use a microchip embedded in the card to authenticate a user's 4 digit PIN. When a user wishes to pay for a product the card is inserted into a small card reader. The reader accesses the chip on the card and the user is asked to enter their 4 digit PIN code. If the codes match, money is deducted from the user's bank account and the product is purchased.

Sensors are devices that measure some physical quantity, converting the information into human useable form. For example, a *thermistor* uses the change in resistivity of a wire to measure temperature. A *thermometer* uses the change in level of mercury to measure temperature. A *photodetector* senses light and is often used to detect when someone or something crosses a beam of light. A *pressure* sensor is often used detect when someone approaches a door which then is instructed to open automatically.

Data logging is the collection of data from one or more sensors at a regular time interval, in some instances over a matter of seconds where perhaps a machine producing engine parts needs continuous monitoring and in other instances over many hours or days where a remote sensor is tracking the movement of ice on a glacier.

Describe each of the following, stating a suitable use for each. [F451 Q3 Jun 2009 (3,3,3)]

MICR

- Magnetic Ink Character Reader/Recognition
- Special characters on document ... are written using magnetisable ink
- Are both computer and human readable

- *Use:* e.g. account numbers on cheques

OCR

- Optical Character Reader/Recognition
- Characters' shapes are scanned ... optically
- Shapes are compared with those stored in computer's memory

- *Use:* e.g. eeading documents into a word processor file

OMR

- Optical Mark Reader/Recognition

- Positions of marks on a document ... equate with information
- Document is scanned for coordinates of marks

- *Use:* e.g. input of lottery choices

OCR is a form of data input. Describe how OCR can be used to help partially sighted people. [F451 Q7 Jan 2011 (2)]

- Used to read printed documents
- Can be used by blind people to read books/mail
- Data output can be turned into speech/enlarged for clearer effect.

Describe the use of two other peripheral devices that would be particularly useful for some disabled people when using a computer. (4)

- Microphone...instructions or data can be read into computer/useful for person without use of hands
- Speakers ...useful for visually impaired people instead of monitor/tells user what the computer has processed.
- Puff-suck switch ... used as digital input/by people who have lost use of limbs

Questions on an examination paper each have four possible answers, labelled A, B, C, D. Explain why optical mark reading (OMR) is a sensible way of marking candidates papers and describe how the marking is done. [F451 Q8 Jun 2010 (5)]

- Correct responses will all be in predetermined positions ...which can be chosen simply by candidates
- Answers are right or wrong
- There are no areas for debate
- Useful statistics produced to inform future examination questions
- Speed of marking
- Accuracy of marking
- Scripts are batch processed
- Positions of shaded areas compared with 'correct' positions
- Number of correct positions added ... and stored in a file according to ... candidate number (which is also shown as shaded areas on paper)

A system for keeping track of goods in a warehouse uses barcode readers to input data about goods going in an out of the warehouse. Describe how a barcode can be used to store data. [F451 Q2 Jan 2009 (3)]

- Patterns of light/dark lines ... pairs of which store digits
- Used to store ID code/used to access record on file
- Different widths/pairs of widths used
- Inclusion of check digit for automatic checking

- Start and stop codes allow bars to be read both ways

Describe how the data can be input to the system from the barcodes. (3)

- Laser/infra red/light used
- Reflections show up (thickness) of lines
- Guide lines to allow reading at an angle
- Check digit calculation done for immediate checking of reading
- Start and stop codes to decide direction of reading … to allow reversal of bars

Describe how the data collected is used to update the information stored about the stock in the warehouse. (4)

- Database has entry for each ID number
- When scanned. ID is found in database
- Number in stock field is … incremented if goods coming in to warehouse
- Decremented if goods going out of warehouse
- Therefore number in stock is always up to date with what is in warehouse

The thickness of sheets of glass produced by a manufacturung process is controlled by a computer which can adjust the distance apart of two rollers between which the glass is rolled. The thickness of the glass coming out from between the rollers is continually monitored by taking readings from sensors arranged above and below the glass. [F451 Q5 Jun 2009]

What is meant by an actuator and how one would be used in this example. (2)

- An actuator is a device which can be operated by a computer/produces physical movement/electric motor
- It would be used to adjust gap between rollers/to control the rate at which the glass is fed through the rollers

The glass is, nominally, 5 mm thick. The sensors measure the thickness and return the readings to the computer. Explain why the processor is not set to maintain the thickness at exactly 5 mm. (2)

- Physical measurement is never exact/unrealistic to expect exactly 5mm/Sensors not precise enough.
- Changes to rollers would occur continuously
- Causing oscillation between > and <

State a sensible range between which the computer attempts to keep the thickness of the glass. (1)

- Any sensible range eg. 5mm +/− 1mm/Symmetric.

Describe how the computer controls the thickness during the rolling process. (5)

- Computer stores parameters between which the thickness is acceptable
- Actual thickness input at regular intervals
- From the sensors
- Actual thickness compared with stored values
- If acceptable then repeat
- Else adjust roller
- Mark for idea of feedback, (If roller adjusted, the next input is compared to previous one to see if it has had an effect)
- If feedback shows that adjustment has had no effect then alarm

The operator of the machine can alter the thickness from 5 mm by inputting a different value to the computer. When the operator inputs new values it is important that the input is verified. Describe how the input can be verified in this example. (2)

- Technician reads value that has been input and ...checks it against value on paper
- Another technician also inputs it or technician inputs value twice
- System checks the two inputs are the same

Patient monitoring in an intensive care ward in a hospital is to be computerised. Important measurements are taken automatically from each of the patients in the ward. State two measurements which will be required and state the hardware required to capture each. [F451 Q5 Specimen Questions (4)]

- Blood pressure ...pressure sensor (on inflatable sleeve)
- Pulse ...pressure device on vein
- Temperature ...thermistor (thermometer)
- Breathing ...sensor on valve in breathing tube

The ward is to be run by one nurse. State two different forms of output which may be used to give the nurse information on the patients. For each format, give an example of its use and state why it is appropriate. (6)

- Sound ...emergency problem (outside parameters)/immediate attention getter
- Light ...problem with specific patient/light can be specific according to location (sound cannot)
- Graphical ...present and recent past measurements/makes for easy trend spotting, visual comparison with parameters
- Reports ...text, hard copy/for archive purposes/to allow analysis of patient condition if an event were to occur

3.6 EXPLAIN THE TECHNIQUES OF VALIDATION AND VERIFICATION

Validation means checking that data is reasonable and complete.Validation checks include the following.
Presence check. Is the data present, has the field required been filled?
Length check. Is the data of a reasonable length, for example is a user name between 5 and 15 characters long?
Format check. Is the data of the correct format? E.g. a date might need to be in the form dd/mm/yyyy
Range check. Is data in the correct range? E.g. a pensioner is someone over the age of 65 and (presumably) younger than say 120.
Existence check. Does the data that has been entered match a previously recorded value. E.g. does entering flight code AZ854 match a flight that actually exists.

Verification means checking that data is consistent. Verification is normally done by visually checking that the data is accurate and by entering a data item twice, for example when creating a new password.

When data is input, it must be verified and validated. When the details of a new customer are input to the system, the data must be verified. Describe one way that the data input can be verified. [F451 Q4 Jun 2011 (2)]

- Double entry/details input twice/checked for any differences/which will be reported for correction
- Visual check/input data on screen checked against data on form/any differences must be corrected

One piece of data that is required by a car insurance company from its customer is the make of car. An existence check and a presence check will be carried out on this data. Describe what is meant by existence check, presence check (2)

- Existence check - checks that the car make exists by checking against a list of possible car makes
- Presence check - checks to ensure that a value has been entered

3.7 DESCRIBE POSSIBLE FORMS OF OUTPUT

Students will be required to draw upon their general knowledge of computing to suggest how and why certain forms of output are to be preferred to others in specific situations. Suppose for example that workers on the shop floor of a car assembly plant need to be trained. Prior to actually inserting an engine into a car it might be wise to learn how to do so from a series of interactive presentations with sound, animations and video showing the process in operation. Members of the management might find it useful to have graphs and reports and perhaps images showing how many cars have been produced in the past six months and how production has varied over that time.

3.8 EXPLAIN THE PROCEDURES INVOLVED IN BACKING UP DATA AND ARCHIVING

Backing up is the regular, frequent (usually at least weekly if not daily) copying of important data to an external device which is then often removed for safe keeping. This means that the data can be restored if the original data is corrupted and damaged in any way.

Archiving is the regular but usually infrequent (possibly every six months or yearly) transfer and then removal from the system of data that is no longer in daily use but must be kept for legal or administrative reasons. Its main purpose is to free up space and improve the speed of access to data still in the system.

The customer and order files used in an office are regularly backed up, while the data produced during operation of the manufacturing process is archived. Describe what is meant backing up files, giving a reason why the customer and order files are backed up. [F451 Q7 Jun 2009 (2,1)]

- Making copy of the data in a file …and the file structure
- On a portable medium
- Kept away from originals
- So that if the original is corrupted it can be replaced

Reason: Customer and order files are very important to the company, so must be protected.

Describe what is meant by archiving data. giving a reason why the data from the manufacturing process is archived. (2,1)

- Storing the data produced …on long term storage
- So that it can be referred to if necessary

Reason: If the process fails then previous data can be searched for evidence. Data is available without taking up space on working storage. Data is available for analysis of manufacturing process.

Workers are paid weekly. Their times at work over the week are collected and the staff file is updated at the same time as the pay is calculated. Describe a backing up routine which could be used for the staff file. (4)

- Back up copy taken weekly ...immediately after updating of staff file
- Multiple copies taken ...and stored in more than 1 location
- At least one is stored off site
- Mention of incremental back up

A student stores all her school work and personal files on her computer. State why the student should back up the data stored on the computer and describe a procedure that the student could follow in order to back up her files. [F451 Q1 Jan 2011 (1,3)]

- Data could become corrupted/disk might crash/data could be lost
- Take a copy of all the files ...onto a removable storage/ solid state storage/ pen drive/ CDRW / DVDRW /online /tape /external or removable HDD
- At a regular interval/e.g. weekly
- Back up kept away from the computer/secure location
- Mention of automatic/incremental backup

Explain the need for companies to back up and archive customer data and the procedures for carrying out these processes. [F451 Q4 Jun 2011 (8)]

This is one of those 8 mark questions that require accurate and appropriate answers. In this instance you will need to explain why companies need to back up and archive data - note these are two quite distinct activities - they are *NOT* the same thing at all. You will then need to explain how they might achieve each of these functions. It's always a good idea before putting pen to paper to try to get clear in your mind the various items or bullet points that you're going to need to make. In this particular question the examiners were looking for the following ...

Need for backup and archive

- Back up necessary in case of corruption of data ...either maliciously or accidentally
- If data destroyed then firm will have to shut
- Archive necessary to keep copy of data for future use
- Frees up space for new material ...by removing little used or redundant data
- Used by firm for mail shots, the following year

Procedure for backup

- Length of time between backups, possibly daily
- Mention of medium used, e.g. DVDRW
- Mention of number of copies, e.g. one kept off site
- Need to keep transaction log between backups
- Incremental backup

Procedure for archive

- At longer intervals, e.g. annually
- Little used data/customers who have not received their policies
- Written to long term storage, e.g. DVDR
- These customers can be removed from current files

Processor components and Peripheral devices

4.1 DESCRIBE THE FUNCTION AND PURPOSE OF THE CONTROL UNIT, MEMORY UNIT AND ARITHMETIC LOGIC UNIT

The *Control unit* is the part of the processor which manages the execution of instructions[1]. It controls all aspects of the Fetch-Decode-Execute cycle. It sends signals to other parts of the computer and synchronises all activity. The *Memory unit* holds user data, the operating system and application programs whilst the computer is in use. The *Arithmetic and Logic Unit* carries out all arithmetic calculations and logical operations. It also manages I/O access to the processor.

Two of the parts of a computer are the memory unit and the ALU. State two items that would be found in the memory unit. [F451 Q6 Specimen Questions (2)]

- Parts of operating system in current use
- Parts of application software in current use
- Data files in current use

State two uses of the ALU. (2)

- To carry out arithmetic operations
- To carry out logical comparisons
- Acts as a gateway to and from the processor

Describe what each of the following parts of a computer does: control unit, memory unit, ALU. [F451 Q4 Jan 2010 (3,3,3)]

Control Unit

- Manages execution of instructions ... by using control signals to other parts of computer

---

[1]BCS Glossary of Computing Terms

- Synchronises actions (using inbuilt clock)
- Controls fetch/execute cycle

Memory Unit

- Stores OS
- Data (currently in use)
- Software (currently in use)/boot program/operations/instructions

ALU

- Carries out arithmetic instructions/calculations
- Carries out logical instructions/decisions
- Acts as a conduit through which all I/O to computer is done/gateway to processor

4.2   EXPLAIN THE NEED FOR, AND USE OF, REGISTERS IN THE FUNCTIONING OF THE PROCESSOR

Microprocessors fetch, decode and execute instructions and data provided by a programmer. Instructions and data need to be stored temporarily whilst they are being used. Registers provide temporary storage space. Some registers are used during the FDE cycle, others are used more generally in the operation of the microprocessor. Registers operate at the speed of the CPU. The names and precise functionality of a particular register differs from microprocessor to microprocessor but their basic purpose and functionality remain the same. The most common are the following.

The *Program Counter* holds the address of the next instruction to be fetched by the CPU.

The *Memory Address Register* holds the address of the location where binary information will be read from or written to.

The *Memory Data Register* holds the data that will be written to or the data that will be read from the address held in the MAR.

The *Current Instruction Register* holds the instruction that is currently being decoded.

The *Accumulator* holds data that is currently being processed,. It stores the result of processing activity such as any arithmetical and logical instructions. In addition, all I/O goes through the accumulator.

In the *Fetch, Decode, Execute* cycle, the contents of the Program Counter are copied into the Memory Address Register and the Program Counter is incremented so as to point to the next instruction. The data held in the address in the Memory Address Register is copied into the Memory Data Register. It is then copied from the Memory Data Register into the Current Instruction Register where it is decoded and executed. The process repeats from the moment the computer is switched on until the moment it is turned off.

A processor contains a number of special registers and buses. Describe the contents of the following special registers: Memory Data Register (MDR), Current Instruction Register (CIR), Accumulator. [F451 Q7 Jun 2011 (2,2,2)]

Memory Data Register (MDR)

- The contents of the address specified in the MAR are copied to the MDR
- This may be an instruction/ operation ...or data to be used (with an instruction)
- It may contain data to be copied to an address

Current Instruction Register (CIR)

- Holds the instruction while it is being decoded/executed
- The contents of MDR are copied into the CIR if it is an instruction
- Operation code as first part of instruction
- Remainder of instruction is address of data to be used in operation or ...the data to be used if immediate operand is used

Accumulator

- Holds the data currently being processed
- Results of processing are stored in the accumulator
- The results of arithmetic carried out in ALU
- All I/O goes through accumulator

Describe two special registers, other than the ALU, which are found in the processor. [F451 Q6 Specimen Questions (2,2)]

- Program Counter (PC)...stores the address of the next instruction
- Memory Address Register...stores the address in memory currently being accessed
- Memory Data Register (MDR)...stores the data being transferred to or from memory
- Current Instruction Register ...stores the instruction currently being operated on

Two of the registers in the functioning of the processor are the MAR (Memory Address Register) and the PC (Program Counter). Describe the contents of the MAR. [F451 Q3 Jan 2009 (2)]

- The position/address in memory …of the location containing either …the next piece of data to be read or …the next instruction to be used.

Explain how the PC is used in the functioning of the processor. (2)

- It stores the address of the next instruction
- It controls the sequence in which the instructions/order in which instructions …are retrieved and executed
- It is incremented after being read
- It is altered as the result of a jump instruction

4.3   Explain the need for, and describe the use of, buses to convey information

There are three essential busses (a parallel group of wires) in any computer system. Data is transferred along the *data bus*. Control signals are sent along the *control bus* and can be used to control the transfer of data. The *address bus* carries the address where any data is to be written to or read from.

Describe the use of different types of bus in the processor. [F451 Q7 Jun 2011 (4)]

- A bus is a parallel group of wires …able to transmit groups of bits together …from one location/register to another in the processor
- Control bus …transmits control signals from the control unit to the rest of the processor
- Address bus …carries the location address to where the data is going
- Data bus …carries the data from one register to another

State three different buses used in a computer system, describing what each is used for. [F451 Q6 Specimen Questions (2,2,2)]

- Data …carries the data/information/two way because direction carried not specified.
- Address …carries information about where the data is being sent to or collected from
- Control …dictates whether the operation is read or write/carried to different parts of processor
- Local …special bus to control flow of large amounts of data, e.g. to the disk drive

Describe <u>two</u> types of bus used for sending transmissions around a processor.
[F451 Q2 Jun 2009 (4)]

- Data bus ... to transmit data between areas of the processor
- Address bus ... to carry address to which the data is being transmitted
- Control bus ... to send control signals from control unit to other parts of the processor

4.4 DESCRIBE THE CONNECTIVITY OF DEVICES (METHODS OF HARD WIRING, AND WIRELESS CONNECTIONS)

There are various methods of connecting devices. *Wired*, examples of which are CAT-5, twisted pair or coaxial. *Wireless* connections use radio waves of various frequencies and operate over relatively short distances of around 100 metres. *Bluetooth* is a wireless connection operating over very short distances of around 5 metres. *Satellites* are used over international distances. *Microwave* links need line of sight, but can operate over quite long distances (many miles). For home and small business use, *infra-red* which operates over short distances of 2 metres and need line of sight.

Peripheral devices are often connected by *serial* cables in which data is sent along a single wire and by *parallel* cables in which data (usually a byte which requires 8 wires) is sent along a group of wires.

Each of these methods have their advantages and disadvantages as highlighted in the questions that follow.

A printer needs to be connected to a computer in order to receive the data that needs to be printed. If devices need to communicate they need to have a method of connection. Describe three methods of connecting devices. [F451 Q3 Jan 2011 (2,2,2)]

- E.g. Wired/cable/copper/coaxial/ Twisted Pair ... description/ interference
- Optical fibre ... transmits data using light beams/interference free
- Infrared ... unobstructed line of sight/example
- Microwave ... used by business to connect network in different locations/line of sight necessary
- Wireless ... used over short distances/not secure because anyone can tap in
- Bluetooth ... wireless communication over very short distances
- Serial, parallel ... description
- Duplex, half duplex ... description

A number of interactive information boards on a seaside promenade are connected in a network which is controlled from the tourist information office on the promenade. State a method of connectivity which could be used and justify your choice. [F451 Q3 Jun 2011 (1,24)]

Either:

- Hard wired/example of cable type
- Communications are not affected by interference
- Terminals are close together (and on a promenade so no obstructions for cable)
- Cables often already exist which can be tapped into

Or:

- Wireless communication
- Terminals are close together and hence are within range
- No infrastructure to be laid down/cheaper infrastructure/vandal proof/not unsightly
- Terminals can be moved at will or others can be inserted as required
- Large volumes of data not required

4.5   DESCRIBE THE DIFFERENCES BETWEEN TYPES OF PRIMARY MEMORY AND EXPLAIN THEIR USES

Random Access Memory (RAM) is volatile, i.e. it loses its data when power is removed. It can be read to and written from. *Read Only Memory (ROM)* is non-volatile, i.e. it does not lose its data when power is switched off. It can be read from but under normal circumstances cannot be written to.

Describe each of the following types of primary memory and state a type of software which would be stored in it. In each case give a reason why the type of memory is appropriate for your choice of software. [F451 Q3 Jan 2009 (3,3)]

ROM (Read Only Memory)

- (Contents of) memory are not erased when power is off/contents cannot be altered

Type of Software:

- Boot program

Reason:

- Program is required immediately power is switched on, therefore must still be there

RAM (Random Access Memory)

- (Contents of) memory is erased when power is off/volatile

Type of Software:

- Applications software/Operating System/User files

Reason:

- Allows changes to be made to saved contents/files in current use/fast access to data

A disk recorder for digital TV signals is controlled by an embedded processor. Explain why the control software is stored on ROM and explain why it will be necessary to have some RAM. [F451 Q3 Jun 2010 (2,2)]

- The control software will not need to be changed
- Cannot be changed
- Will not need loading/installing
- Immediately available when switched on

We need RAM because ...

- Need to allow user to enter data
- Processor must have some RAM as working memory/buffer
- Used to load data from disk when playing/currently running programs/data in use

4.6   DESCRIBE THE BASIC FEATURES, ADVANTAGES, DISADVANTAGES AND USES OF SECONDARY STORAGE MEDIA

Hard disks are magnetic and typically hold many gigabytes or more recently, terabytes of storage space. They are slow compared to RAM. They can be physically quite large, though 1" drives are now very common. They are used to store the operating system, application programs and user data when the computer is not in use.

CD/DVD. These use optical technologies. CDs typically hold around 800MB which is quite small these days and have been widely superseded by DVDs which can hold 8.5 GB and Blu-Ray which can hold up to 50 GB on dual-layer discs. Optical storage is relatively slow compared to hard disks.

Solid state memory devices such as memory sticks can commonly hold up to 64GB and are increasing in storage capacity all the time. They are fast, relatively inexpensive and can be extremely small, ideal for use in cameras and mobile phones.

4.7   DESCRIBE THE TRANSFER OF DATA BETWEEN DIFFERENT DEVICES AND PRIMARY MEMORY, INCLUDING THE USES OF BUFFERS AND INTERRUPTS

Describe the use of interrupts and buffers when data is transferred from primary memory to a storage device. [F451 Q1 Jan 2009 (4)]

- Data sent to buffer from primary memory
- Interrupt sent when buffer is full
- Buffer is emptied to storage device
- At slower speed, to accommodate device
- When buffer is empty ... an interrupt is sent to processor
- To request buffer refill

Describe the transfer of a file of data from primary memory to a storage device. [F451 Q2 Jan 2010]
Physical:

- Buffer ... a temporary storage
- Interrupt ... message sent to processor/control unit
- Type of communication medium
- Serial/parallel communication

Logical:

- Buffer filled by primary memory
- Processor can continue other tasks
- Buffer emptied to storage
- Interrupt sent to request buffer is refilled
- Interrupt priority compared with priority of present task
- Use of priority to assign interrupt with position in queue
- Data arranged in packets/blocks
- Data error checked on arrival
- Method of error checking explained

4.8 DESCRIBE A RANGE OF COMMON PERIPHERAL DEVICES IN TERMS OF THEIR FEATURES, ADVANTAGES, DISADVANTAGES AND USES

Questions that fall under this section require the student to draw upon his or general general knowledge of computing. There are situations under which various types of readers are appropriate, for example bar code readers (product checkout in supermarkets, bookshops etc.), MICR readers (banking), OCR (scanning of text), OMR (multiple choice exam questions).

Printers are used in wide variety of situations ranging from home (ink jet, good text, high resolution photographs, general printing) and school use (laser printers, high quality, high use) to product checkouts (receipt printing using simple ink jets and occasionally dot-matrix). Plotters are high quality multiple pen, one pen at a time devices for drawing lines on wide (Ao and sometimes larger) and long (potentially many metres) paper. Use is usually confined to Computer Aided Design/Computer Aided Manufacture (CAD/CAM) applications in areas such as architecture and engineering design. Speakers can range from those attached to your PC to extremely loud sirens used in high noise factory environments as danger signals. Similarly microphones can be simple devices used to Skype family and friends to high quality devices costing many thousands of pounds used in the music industry.

Sensors are devices that measure some physical quantity which is then converted into a signal that can be read by a computer or a person. There are hundreds of different types of sensors ranging from *thermistors* (a resistor whose resistance varies according to temperature) and *proximity* sensors common now in cars to indicate when you are too close to a nearby car, to the *breathalyser* used to indicate whether someone has drunk too much alcohol to drive safely.

Actuators convert a source of energy into motion. Energy can be provided by electricity (electric motors), by air (pneumatic cylinders - manufacturing) and by fluids (hydraulic cylinders - damping systems in cars). Motion can be rotary (turning wheels), linear (driving pistons) or oscillatory (piezoelectric).

4.9   DESCRIBE AND JUSTIFY THE APPROPRIATE PERIPHERAL HARDWARE FOR A GIVEN APPLICATION

A seaside town has a number of interactive information boards placed at intervals along the promenade. The purpose of the boards is to provide information to holidaymakers. A user might search for entertainment available or reasonably priced guest houses that have vacancies. State two peripherals which would be used at each site, justifying your answers. [F451 Q3 Jun 2011 (2,2)]

- Touch sensitive screen (allow screen/monitor/VDU) ... simple to use/less susceptible to vandalism/can cope with weather
- Printer ... to output hard copy of results of search (to be taken away)
- Disk drive ... to allow storage of data

Data transmission

5.1 DESCRIBE THE CHARACTERISTICS OF A LOCAL AREA NETWORK AND A WIDE AREA NETWORK

A *Local Area Network (LAN)* covers a small geographical area and is usually wired or short range wireless and is reasonably secure if set up correctly. A *Wide Area Network (WAN)* covers a large geographical area, uses the internet or long distance links, microwave if line of sight, possibly satellite for international, and needs additional hardware such as modems. WANs are potentially less secure.

State three differences between a LAN and a WAN. [F451 Q6 Jan 2011 (2)]

- LAN is one site/WAN geographically remote
- LAN is hard wired or wireless from central point/WAN tends to use external communications
- LAN more secure/WAN subject to attack
- LAN requires no extra communication device/WAN requires modem

Describe the characteristics of Local Area and Wide Area Networks (LANS and WANs). [F451 Q8 Jun 2009 (3)]

- LAN over small area
- WAN remote
- Different forms of communication media
- LAN is more secure
- Data on a WAN is subject to interception

5.2 SHOW AN UNDERSTANDING OF THE HARDWARE AND SOFTWARE NEEDED FOR A LOCAL AREA NETWORK AND FOR ACCESSING A WIDE AREA NETWORK

LANs use routers, switches, hubs, network cards and a Network Operating System (NOS) - built into all modern operating systems. WANs need routers, modems and either telephone cabling or fibre optic cable if they are to use the internet.

A small business has a number of stand-along computers in an office. State <u>two</u> items of software and <u>two</u> items of hardware which may be used to network them. [F451 Q7 Jan 2009 (4)]
Software:

- Network Operating System
- Drivers for hardware
- Network versions of applications software
- Communications software

Hardware:

- Network interface cards
- Cabling/or other communication medium/wireless access points
- Server/File server/hub/switch

State how the medium used for communication will alter if the computers are to be linked to the internet. (2)

- Fibre optic cable
- Telephone cable I
- Infra red/microwave/satellite
- Need for a modem/router

Explain the meaning of the term transparency in a network operating system. [F451 Q7 Specimen Questions (2)]

- Actions which are taken by the O.S ... without the user being aware of them
- If the network is transparent then the user is unaware ... of being on a network terminal ... believing it to be a P.C./unaware of other users

Explain how printing is carried out by a network operating system when there is only one printer available. [F451 Q7 Specimen Questions (3)]

- May use a print server to control the operations
- Jobs are sent to the print spooler ... which stores each job as a file ... and references to the file in a print queue

- When printer is free the next job referenced in the queue is sent to the printer from the file.

5.3 DESCRIBE THE DIFFERENT TYPES OF DATA TRANSMISSION: SERIAL AND PARALLEL; AND SIMPLEX, HALF-DUPLEX AND DUPLEX MODES

Serial transmission is one bit at a time (often along a single wire). *Parallel* transmission uses multiple wires and can send multiple bits (usually 8 making up one byte, one wire per bit) simultaneously. *Simplex* transmission means that data can only be transferred in one direction. *Half Duplex* transmission means that data can be transferred in both directions, but *not* at the same time. *Full duplex* transmissions mean that data can be transferred in both directions simultaneously.

When data is transmitted from one location to another, different types of data transmission can be used. Describe the difference between serial and parallel data transmission. [F451 Q2 Jun 2009 (2)]

- Serial is one bit transmitted at a time/single wire
- Parallel is multiple bits transmitted at a time/many wires

Describe the difference between half duplex and duplex transmission. (2)

- Half duplex is communication in both directions but one at a time
- Duplex is communication in both directions simultaneously

State a computer application which may use parallel data transmission, justifying your answer. [F451 Q2 Jun 2011 (2)]

Application

- Sending data from hard drive to the processor
- Send data from a games console to the processor
- Video streaming
- Sending data from the processor to the graphics card

Justification

- Speed of devices - i.e. devices are fast, they can and should receive data quickly
- Volume of data is great so to save time we need to send it quickly
- Time sensitivity of data

5.4   EXPLAIN THE RELATIONSHIP BETWEEN BIT RATES AND THE TIME SENSITIVITY OF THE INFORMATION

Bit rate refers to the number of bits that can be transferred per second. This is often referred to as the *Baud* rate. Typical data transfer speeds throughout LANs are 100 MBits per second or 1 GBits per second. Currently, typical internal access speeds are around 10 MBits per second. Clearly if you are trying to transfer a lot of data, higher bit rates are desirable and often essential.

Describe what is meant by the bit rate of data transmission. [F451 Q7 Jan 2010 (2)]

- The rate at which data is transferred (NOT speed)/how many bits in a specific time period ... measured in bits per second/baud
- Actual rate of data transmission can vary because of other factors like the need to transmit control signals

State a type of data transmission which would require a high bit rate, giving reasons for your choice. (3)

- Streaming of a video to a machine
- Large amount of data
- Time sensitive because ... delay will interrupt video output

A network is used for sending word processed documents from one machine to another so that they can be proof read the following day. It is also used to transmit video files for viewing by all network users simultaneously as part of a training program. Explain how these two uses influence the bit rate used across the network. [F451 Q9 Jan 2011 (4)]

- Word processed documents tend to have less data to transmit than a video file as they are smaller
- Word processed documents not needed immediately
- Bit rate for word processed documents unimportant because there is time for data to download even at slow rate
- Video file large/used immediately ... therefore data is time sensitive ... therefore requires a high bit rate or data becomes useless

Some of the files used in an office are simple text files used by people who deal with customer orders. The reception area has a computer screen where customers can enquire about the company and watch videos which are streamed direct from a storage device on the network. Explain why text files and streamed video may use different bit rates. [F451 Q7 Jan 2009 (3)]

- Text files use a small volume of data/Videos require large volume of data

- These need to be sent in a small period of time if video is to be seen in real time/it will freeze or lag otherwise
- Consequently, number of bits per second is important/dependent on the data being sent
- Video data is time sensitive

5.5 RECOGNISE THAT ERRORS CAN OCCUR IN DATA TRANSMISSION, AND EXPLAIN METHODS OF DETECTING AND CORRECTING THESE ERRORS

Errors will often occur when transferring data. Methods of detecting and correcting include the following.

Parity checking. This is when one bit in every byte (perhaps the most significant bit, or more usually an extra bit) is added to the word thus ensuring the the total number of 1s in the byte is even (for even parity) or odd (if using odd parity). If a byte is being sent with even parity and when received, is found to contain an odd number of ones, the receiver will ask the sender to re-send the offending byte.

Echoing. An inefficient but occasionally used method is for the receiver to simply echo back to the sender everything that is sent. If the sender doesn't get back what it sent, it re-sends the byte.

Checksum. A checksum is a mathematical calculation carried out on a packet of data. The result of the calculation is added to the packet and sent to the recipient. The recipient carries out the same calculation on the data and checks to see whether it's result is the same as the checksum it has received. If not it asks for the packet to be re-sent.

Describe how an echo can be used to check for errors in data transmission. [F451 Q3 Specimen Questions (3)]

- Data is sent back to origin ... where it is compared to original
- Any differences will signify a transmission error
- The original data is re-sent.

Describe two alternative error checking methods which may be used when data is being transmitted across a network. (2,2)

- *Parity check*
- An extra bit added to data byte ... which makes the number of ones in the byte either always odd or always even

- *Checksum*
- The data bytes are added together ignoring any overflow
- The calculation can be repeated at the destination and compared with the transmitted sum.

Errors may occur during data transmission. Two methods of checking for these errors are check sums and parity checks. Explain how a check sum is used to check transmitted data for errors. [F451 Q8 Jun 2009 (4)]

- Blocks of bytes are added before transmission ...to give a total, with carries out of the total ignored
- This total is transmitted with the block
- The same calculation is done on the data blocks at the destination
- And result is compared with the transmitted value ...if different, there is a transmission error

Parity bits can be used to check for errors in transmission and may also be used to check and self-correct data in blocks. Explain how parity checks of data blocks can sometimes be used to correct transmission errors automatically. (4)

- Each byte has a parity bit
- Each bit place has also got a parity bit
- All parity is checked
- If there is an error in the parity for a byte and the parity for a place value
- Then where they intersect will be the faulty bit
- If it is 0, change it to 1/If it is 1 change it to 0
- If more than one error in block then data is re-transmitted

One error checking method is to use parity. One of the following bytes has been corrupted in transmission. 00010010 01011101 10101001 11000011. State which the corrupt byte is and explain why it is corrupt. [F451 Q1 Jun 2010 (3)]

- 01011101/2nd byte
- Has an odd number of ones
- All others have an even number of ones/even parity

5.6   DESCRIBE PACKET SWITCHING AND CIRCUIT SWITCHING

Packet switching is the use of fixed size packets of data together with address and control information. All data on the internet is encapsulated in packets. Packets are typically around 1,500 bytes in size. All emails, web pages, image data, downloadable programs and voice over IP conversations are split up and made into packets. Each packet is sent individually onto the internet and is routed according to its address information to its destination. Packets of any given piece of data may well follow different paths. At the destination, the packets are re-ordered and re-assembled into the original message. If packets are missing or damaged (identified by an incorrect checksum), the recipient will ask the sender to re-send the necessary information.

Circuit switching also uses packets but packets are sent one after the other along a pre-established route to the destination. There is a need to re-assemble, but no need to re-order packets at the destination. Packet switching is inherently more secure than circuit switching because it is difficult to guarantee intercepting all data packets (since there is no guaranteed route from sender to recipient).

Describe packet switching to send data from one device to another on a network. [F451 Q8 Jun 2011 (5)]

- Data divided into packets of equal sizes
- Each packet has a label attached stating ...destination...what the data file is ...which packet number it is ...transmitting addresses
- Individual packets sent on to network to follow most convenient path
- Packets follow different routes/no preset path
- Packets arrive in random order
- Packets must be reordered
- Reasonably secure

When data is transmitted between machines on a network, the data can be sent using either packet switching or circuit switching. Describe what is meant by packet switching, circuit switching and finally, give one advantage and one disadvantage of using packet switching rather than circuit switching. [F451 Q2 Jan 2010 (2,2,2)]

Packet switching

- Packets sent onto network
- Find their own routes to destination/use different routes
- Packets must be reordered at destination/arrives in wrong order
- Packets have identity on label

Circuit switching

- Route reserved before transmission ...for the duration of the transmission
- All packets follow same route/in order
- Packets must be reassembled at destination/arrives in order

Advantage:

- Does not tie up a proportion of the network/Secure because impossible to intercept all packets.

- Loss of part of communication will not be fatal/if message does not arrive safely only one packet needs to be resent

Disadvantage:

- Must be reordered at destination/only as fast as its slowest packet

Describe how a file of data can be transmitted from one machine to another across a WAN using packet switching. [F451 Q3 Specimen Questions (5)]

- File divided into groups of bits (packets) ... of standard size
- Made up of control bits, data and destination address
- Packets are individually sent across the network
- Across different routes
- Packets must be ordered at destination to recreate data

5.7   EXPLAIN THE DIFFERENCE IN USE OF PACKET SWITCHING AND CIRCUIT SWITCHING

Explain the differences between using packet switching and circuit switching to transmit a message. [F451 Q2 Jun 2009 (3)]

- PS has no established route/CS establishes a route along which to send packets
- PS means packets being sent on individual routes/CS has packets all on same route
- PS message cannot be (easily) intercepted/CS message can because all on same route
- PS packets need to be reordered/CS packets remain in correct order
- PS maximises use of network/CS ties up large areas of network

5.8   DEFINE THE TERM PROTOCOL AND EXPLAIN THE IMPORTANCE OF A PROTOCOL TO THE TRANSMISSION OF DATA

Communication protocols establish the rules by which two devices can communicate.

Data is communicated between devices in a network. A protocol is needed in a network. State what is meant by a protocol. [F451 Q8 Jun 2011 (2)]

- A set of rules ... to govern transmission of data

Describe three parts of a protocol which would be necessary to allow communication in a network. (2,2,2)

- Bit rate ...to ensure sender and receiver are sending and receiving data at the same rate/measured in bits per second
- Error checking/devices...must agree on method, e.g. even or odd parity/otherwise messages will never be accepted
- Character set used ...otherwise binary codes would relate to other characters than those intended
- What type of data transmission is used ...serial or parallel/simplex or duplex/packet size

Explain why a handshake signal is necessary. [F451 Q7 Jan 2010 (3)]

- To ensure that both devices are ready for data transmission/want to communicate/establish a link
- To ensure that same protocol/rules are being used
- To ensure synchronisation of signal
- To agree error detection rules other sensible part of protocol

Explain why the protocol used to create an interface between two devices is layered. [F451 Q9 Jan 2011 (3)]

- Enables manufacturers to design for a particular layer
- Layers are ordered ...which simplifies the creation of the protocol
- Changes can be made by altering a single layer ...and the links to the other layers in contact with it

Explain how communication links are established between devices. [F451 Q6 Jan 2009 (3)]

- A handshake signal sent from one device ...and acknowledged by the other
- This states that each is now ready for communication
- Establishment of medium for communication
- Mention of one part of protocol being established: Parity/async or sync/baud rate

Explain the use of http in the transfer of data across the internet. [F451 Q3 Specimen Questions (2)]

- A protocol ...which controls the transmission of web pages
- Identifies the address of a web page
- Designed to handle the links within the page

5.9 DESCRIBE THE NEED FOR COMMUNICATION BETWEEN DEVICES AND BETWEEN COMPUTERS, AND EXPLAIN THE NEED FOR PROTOCOLS TO ESTABLISH COMMUNICATION LINKS

Protocols are essential to ensure that two devices can communicate successfully. Such things as an agreed speed of transmission, whether handshaking (the agreement between two devices covering who is sending and when) is to be done in hardware or software, whether parity is to be used, and if so, whether even or odd are essential before two devices can communicate.

5.10 EXPLAIN THE NEED FOR BOTH PHYSICAL AND LOGICAL PROTOCOLS AND THE NEED FOR LAYERING IN AN INTERFACE

Logical protocols include baud rate, handshaking, parity, number of stop and start bits. *Physical protocols* include wireless or wired, CAT-5 or twisted pair, microwave or infra-red.

Hardware protocols are needed to ensure that two devices are physically capable of exchanging information. Logical protocols are needed to ensure that the format of the data together with any higher level functionality such as packet sizes, encryption algorithms used and so on are agreed and used by both devices.

Protocols consist of both physical and logical parts. Describe the physical parts of a protocol, the logical parts of a protocol. [F451 Q6 Jan 2009 (3,3)]

Physical:

- Descriptions of the physical connections between the devices
- Wireless or hard-wired?
- What frequencies?
- Serial or parallel?
- Radio or microwave?
- Copper cable or fibre optic?

Logical:

- Baud rate
- Error correction technique
- Routing
- Flow control/synchronisation of messages
- Descriptions of the rules governing the data
- Packet size

- Compression techniques
- Encryption algorithms
- Digital signatures

Implications of computer use

6.1 Discuss changing trends in computer use and their economic, social, legal and ethical effects on society

A programmer used to go to the office every day and work there. State an advantage and a disadvantage of working from home for each of: the programmer, the software house, society. [F451 Q9 Jun 2010 (2,2,2)]

The programmer

- More freedom with family
- Save money/time on commuting
- More easily distracted
- Lack of social contact
- Difficulty if system malfunctions/problem met/team communication more difficult

The software house

- Do not need to supply offices/car parking spaces/less expensive to run offices
- Work can be outsourced easily
- Less control over work of individuals
- More difficulty in altering course of work/less flexible

Society

- Less pollution from travelling/less traffic congestion
- Less infrastructure required
- Opportunities for employment of disabled people
- Less need for coalescing in cities
- Reduction in service industries
- Less structure in society

Explain the need for legislation to govern the use of computers for storing personal data. [F451 Q3 Jan 2010 (4)]

- Information is confidential ...and sensitive
- Information must be accurate
- Clients must have confidence that measures are taken to protect their data
- Data stored must be refreshed regularly to ensure irrelevant data is not kept
- Need to protect the unwary
- Worry about identity theft ...or fraud
- Stop data being passed on

The internet has had a major effect on society. Discuss the social and ethical effects on young people of allowing unrestricted access to the internet. [F451 Q2 Jun 2009 (8)]

Another 8 mark question where the quality of your written communication will be assessed. The examiners expected your answer to contain the following points ...

Social:

- Less socialising because on computer all the time
- Sees other societies which will cause friction with ...parents and other figures of authority
- Will raise expectations/wants
- Will increase knowledge of other societies ...and give opportunity to learn about others/communicate directly

Ethical:

- Use of other peoples work
- Copyright
- Plagiarism
- Use for educational purposes
- Use to spread understanding

6.2   EXPLAIN CHANGES TO SOCIETY BROUGHT ABOUT BY THE USE OF COMPUTER SYSTEMS

Until recently a loans system at a local library had been a manual one. Explain the likely changes to the staffs work expectations following the introduction of the computerised system. [F451 Q5 Jan 2010 (5)]

- Worry about job loss

- Worry about competence/training
- Less time spent on mundane tasks/more time on interesting things like research and helping public
- More information available/available when needed
- Change of stress levels
- More chances of improved qualifications/training makes workers more skilled
- Enhanced job prospects/more pay
- Expected to be more literate with system
- Increased work load to bring new system on line

A ward at a local hospital is to be computerised. Discuss the likely effects of this computerisation on the people involved. (8)

- Nurse needs training
- May be unable to adapt to new work practices
- May qualify for promotion/increased pay because of better qualifications
- May be redundancy issue
- Patients/relatives may be concerned about lack of human contact
- Lower standard of care because of reliance on machines
- Conversely, may be happier because of reduction in chance of human error
- Reduction in staff may jeopardise care if more than 1 patient goes critical
- Saving of costs may result in more patients/wards possible
- Reduced waiting times as a result of the above
- Nurse given far more responsibility
- May have problem in accepting so much responsibility easier if decisions are shared

6.3 DISCUSS THE EFFECTS ON PRIVACY AND CONFIDENTIALITY OF DATA HELD IN COMPUTER SYSTEMS

A supermarket stores data about customers who have loyalty cards. Explain why some customers may be concerned about giving their personal details to the supermarket. [F451 Q5 Jun 2011 (2)]

- Information can be looked at by others
- Information may be hacked/worries about privacy
- Data can be used to commit fraud/steal from accounts
- Worries created by reports in the press
- Information may be sold on/passed on
- Information used to send junk mail
- Customer does not know what use may be made of the data

Describe steps the supermarket can take to reassure customers about their concerns. (5)

- Passwords on system
- Passwords allow access to only a few staff
- Staff who are allowed access need to be stated (and reported to the DPregistrar)
- Computer systems protected by firewalls/anti-hacking measures
- Physical access restricted
- Data encrypted
- Out of date data is deleted
- Customer can inspect details on request
- Reassure customers by advertising measures that have been taken
- Opt-out of marketing tick box

A major use of data transmission is in communicating with other sources over the internet. Use of the internet can affect the privacy and confidentiality of data held in a computer system. Describe THREE steps which can be taken to protect data held in a computer system. [F451 Q6 Jun 2010 (2,2,2)]

- Passwords ... restrict access to system/files/keep secure by using mixture of cases/characters
- Use of a firewall ... to stop signals from unauthorised users reaching the system/hardware or software
- Encryption ... so that if unauthorised access is gained the data is unintelligible
- Proxy server ... restricts the users allowed access to individual machines on network
- Intrusion detection system ... warns when uninvited access is attempted

Discuss the effects on the confidentiality of data when it is held on computer systems and steps which can be taken to protect the confidentiality of the data. [F451 Q5 Jan 2011 (8)]

Another 8 mark question where your written communication skills will be assessed. The examiners are expecting you to have made the following points ...

Positive points

- The data is not readable without access to a computer
- The data is not stored in human readable form
- Easier to log who has accessed the data

Negative points

- The files of data can be easily and quickly copied

- Copies of data can be placed on media or sent elsewhere electronically
- Searches for specific data to steal can be made easily and quickly
- Systems can be hacked and data looked at remotely
- More difficult to restrict number of copies of data in circulation

Measures which can be taken

- Passwords to gain access to system
- Passwords to access files
- Encryption of data
- Firewalls to restrict access to systems
- Physical measures to restrict access
- Proxy server to restrict users allowed access to individual machines on network from internet
- Intrusion detection system to warn when uninvited access is attempted

6.4 UNDERSTAND THE NEED FOR LEGISLATION GOVERNING COMPUTER USE

This part of the specification requires you to have a broader, more general understanding of computing systems. Questions in this area are likely to assume that at the very least you are familiar with the data protection act of 1998.

With the all pervasive nature of computer systems in daily life there are many situations where the use of computer systems might very well require legislation. As a very simple example, presumably we'd like to limit the gathering of personal information to that which society regards as essential but no more. Confidentiality and privacy are protected by the law and in response to a growing unease amongst people about how their private data might be being used, in 1998 the government passed the data protection act regarding personal data which amongst very much else, says the following about personal information.

1. Personal data shall be obtained only for one or more specified and lawful purposes, and shall not be further processed in any manner incompatible with that purpose or those purposes

2. Personal data shall be adequate, relevant and not excessive in relation to the purpose or purposes for which they are processed

3. Personal data shall be accurate and, where necessary, kept up to date

4. Personal data processed for any purpose or purposes shall not be kept for longer than is necessary for that purpose or those purposes

5. Personal data shall be processed in accordance with the rights of data subjects under this Act

6. Appropriate technical and organisational measures shall be taken against unauthorised or unlawful processing of personal data and against accidental loss or destruction of, or damage to, personal data

7. Personal data shall not be transferred to a country or territory outside the European Economic Area unless that country or territory ensures an adequate level of protection for the rights and freedoms of data subjects in relation to the processing of personal data.

There have been a number of high profile cases in the media where web sites distributing a wide variety of audio and visual media have been prosecuted and forced to shut down. The law is often slow in realising the potential of the Internet for delivery of such media and society needs to decide exactly what is and what is not permitted. What society in the shape of politicians decides should not be permitted is then enacted in law.

Index

Lightning Source UK Ltd.
Milton Keynes UK
UKOW04f1856290414

230826UK00008B/259/P